PRIESTS IN LOVE WITH GOD

Archbishop Alfred C. Hughes, S.T.D.

Priests in Love
with God
and Eager to Witness
to the Gospel

With a Foreword by
Bishop Robert Barron, S.T.D.

IGNATIUS PRESS   SAN FRANCISCO

"*Feed My Sheep*"
Jesus instructs Saint Peter
Mosaic by Bodley and Gardner (end of 19th century)
St. Barnabas church, London
©istock/sedmak

Cover design by Roxanne Mei Lum

© 2021 by Ignatius Press, San Francisco
All rights reserved
ISBN 978-1-62164-478-1 (PB)
ISBN 978-1-64229-185-8 (eBook)
Library of Congress Control Number 2021936852
Printed in the United States of America ♾

CONTENTS

FOREWORD

By Bishop Robert Barron, S.T.D.

The clerical sexual abuse crisis, which initially broke in 2002 and exploded again with shocking clarity in 2018, has largely corroded the credibility of the Catholic Church and left countless lives in ruins. But as I pointed out in *Letter to a Suffering Church*,[1] the Church has passed through great scandals before—up to and including at the level of the papacy itself—and she has survived. We have grounds for hope. That hope is found, however, not in institutional reform, psychological analysis, or new programs and protocols—important though all of these are. It is found, rather, in a return to Jesus Christ and a recovery of a radical form of the Christian life. In short, we must get back to basics.

This Christocentric renewal must, of course, include laymen. But a renewal of the priesthood and a rededication to its ideals are imperative. A priest is, first and foremost, one who belongs to Jesus Christ; everything he is and has—including his mind and his body, his words and his deeds, his private and public life—must be given to the Lord. A priest is also a "soul doctor"—that is, one who reaches and heals the still-point at the heart of every person, that point of encounter with the living God. And in and through his self-gift to the Lord in his role as soul doctor, the priest is a missionary of the Gospel, one who

---

[1] Robert Barron, *Letter to a Suffering Church: A Bishop Speaks on the Sexual Abuse Crisis* (Park Ridge, IL: Word on Fire, 2019).

acts *in Persona Christi* to the wider world and offers healing precisely through the healing of the baptized.

Priests in Love with God and Eager to Witness to the Gospel by Archbishop Hughes marks an important step toward this spiritual renewal of the priesthood. It's a brief but invigorating book that should be read by, and recommended to, any man—especially any young man—discerning or entering the priesthood. One of the things that stays in my mind from the general sessions of the 2018 Synod on Young People, the Faith, and Vocational Discernment was a statement from one of the young people there who said in reference to priests and bishops: "We don't want bureaucrats; we want fathers." This is precisely how Archbishop Hughes approaches his reader—not as a polished bureaucrat but as a spiritual father.

Rooted in the lessons of history and the saints and woven together with prayer, he calls present and future ministers of the Church back to the transformative basics of the priesthood: to a heroic life of self-emptying, self-sacrifice, and self-gift; to a keen awareness of our own fallenness and an alertness to the dangers of clericalism; to being grounded in the Eucharist and eager to proclaim the Gospel; to both ascetic discipline and joyful witness; to both pastoral care and the pursuit of truth; to an understanding of the ministerial priesthood as serving the priesthood of the baptized; and, critically, to a priesthood that evangelizes the culture. But Archbishop Hughes knows that the key to all of this— and the key to renewal of the Church in our time—is finally relying on the all-powerful Creator rather than our own creaturely powers. "The Church needs God!" he exhorts at the beginning of Chapter 14. "The Church needs to seek God, kneel in adoration before God, love God above all, and become more fully an icon of God's presence to the world."

In recent years I have come to a deeper appreciation of St. Augustine's insight on the very first page of his *Confessions*: "Our hearts are made for you, O God, and they will not rest until they rest in you."[2] For the man discerning or embarking on a vocation to the priesthood and anxious and worried about many things, this spiritual formula is especially instructive. So before leaving the reader to Archbishop Hughes, I would like to underscore, as a conclusion to these remarks, the prayer from his chapter on St. Augustine (Chapter 4): "Lord Jesus, who have called me to make a sacrificial gift of myself and to resist selfish behavior in order to serve your Church, help me through the intercession of St. Augustine to realize that gift in my own life and to assist others to choose you above all else in their lives. Grant this in your own name. Amen."

[2] Augustine, *Confessions* I, 1, trans. John Ryan (New York: Doubleday Image, 1960).

INTRODUCTION

Bishop Robert Barron released in the summer of 2019 his *Letter to a Suffering Church*.[1] He is a particularly gifted evangelizer who has his finger on the pulse of young adults. He appreciates the challenges they face. He engages them quite fruitfully in conversation by utilizing the social media in which they are so much at home. In this *Letter*, Bishop Barron is unafraid to acknowledge all that has gone awry in the clergy sex abuse scandal and the sometimes inept way in which bishops have handled it. He then draws effectively on Sacred Scripture and Church history to provide insight and context for his message. That message is an impassioned plea to remain faithful to the Church that hands on such incredible divine treasures in earthen vessels in order to fight ardently for the reform and renewal that the Church needs.

This message speaks powerfully to people of all ages. Ever since relinquishing responsibilities as Archbishop of New Orleans, I have experienced the privilege of serving on the faculty of Notre Dame Seminary as an adjunct professor and spiritual director. I have been invigorated and inspired by the men who are presenting themselves as candidates for the priesthood, despite the challenging and difficult news that envelops them. They, of course, struggle to discern and then embrace the vocation to the priesthood. Those who persevere want to make a difference and want to work with others who are willing to make a difference.

---

[1] Robert Barron, *Letter to a Suffering Church: A Bishop Speaks on the Sexual Abuse Crisis* (Park Ridge, IL: Word on Fire, 2019).

In June 2017 Elizabeth Dias, a regular contributor to *Time* magazine, wrote a cover story entitled "The God Squad".[2] She had interviewed a number of those who were being ordained that year from diverse seminaries. She was encouraged to discover that they were men who came from quite varied ethnic, racial, and professional backgrounds, but they had fallen in love with the Lord and were on fire with a desire to bring the Gospel message to the world. They were unafraid to venture to the peripheries of Church life or even of human life to find those in spiritual need. She described them as informed about doctrine, yet pastorally attuned. She did not find it easy to categorize them as politically conservative or liberal. She recognized that they could be open in their struggles with chastity in a hypersexualized world, but still willing to commit themselves to celibate life. These candidates were savvy about the use of social media. This depiction of the candidates for the priesthood, although it does not capture all the variations, resonates with my experience as well—and provides an encouraging counterpoint to the fallout from the scandal.

All of this prompts me to enter the fray in an effort to contribute to the spiritual renewal of bishops, priests, and seminarians. The greatest antidote to sin and scandal is holiness of life. Although all the baptized are called to holiness of life, there is a special need and importance for holy priests today. In every era in the Church, when spiritual renewal was desperately needed, it was saints who led the way. A number of them were holy priests or bishops.

In this book I propose to draw from the Church's rich resources in Sacred Scripture and Sacred Tradition to explore what have been some of the challenging moments

---

[2] Elizabeth Dias, "The God Squad", *Time*, June 19, 2017, 34–41.

for the priesthood in Church history, and what saints have done to help raise up genuinely holy bishops and priests in response to the difficulties of their own time. It is my hope that these reflections will help suggest an approach beyond a mere disciplinary reform toward that spiritual renewal which will invite more people to see God and seek salvation in and through his Church.

Chapter 1

The New Testament Testimony: Stumbling Disciples Become Spirit-Filled Apostles

Stumbling Apostles

The place to begin has to be with the inspired Word of God. The Baptism of Jesus in the Jordan River (Mt 3:13–17; Mk 1:9–11; Lk 3:21–22; Jn 1:31–34) was both the highlight of the prophetic ministry of John the Baptist and the starting point for the public ministry of Jesus Christ. The Father spoke in affirmation of his Son, and the Holy Spirit appeared in the form of a dove. From that moment, Jesus began to invite special disciples to accompany him (Mt 4:18–22; Mk 1:16–20; Lk 5:1–11; Jn 1:35–51), while also engaging in a Galilean ministry of proclaiming to all who listened that the time of prophecy was being fulfilled in him (Mt 4:12–17; Mk 1:14–15 cf. Lk 4:14–15). The kingdom of God was at hand! In the early stages of this public ministry in Galilee, Jesus reached out to the crowds that gathered to hear him. But after choosing twelve from among the growing number of disciples (Mt 10:1–4; Mk 3:13–19; Lk 6:12–16), he seemed to focus more and more on their formation.

This shift of attention could not have been easy for Jesus! He had not chosen accomplished men. He bypassed the Levitical priests, the prophets, the Pharisees, and the Scribes—those who had studied, prayed, and learned the ways of God. Rather, he chose a few fishermen, a tax collector, a mixed-up zealot and a thief. Even though they were mysteriously drawn to him, they seemed disappointingly slow to discern who he really was or the deeper meaning of his mission and message.

These men were more inclined to envision the kingdom of God as a restoration of the Kingdom of Israel, freeing the Jews from the despised Roman rule. They even hoped to enjoy privileged places in that kingdom (Mk 10:35–45). They rejoiced when given a role of exorcising demons but seemed inclined to regard it as personal power, rather than a gift from God (Lk 10:17–20). They failed to appreciate the need for fasting or self-abnegation in winning a victory over certain demons (Mk 9:14–29). They marveled at Jesus' miracles but were inclined to interpret them as physical healings rather than signs pointing to deeper realities—for example, when Jesus healed the paralytic (Mt 9:1–8; Mk 2:1–12; Lk 5:17–26). Although Jesus had tried to prepare them for his Passion and Death with numerous predictions, they scattered when the arrest took place in the Garden of Gethsemane (Mt 26:56; Mk 14:50). Only John had the courage to reappear on Calvary (Jn 19:26).

Even after the Resurrection, these same apostles struggled to believe. Thomas demanded scientific proof (Jn 20:24–29). Others of them tried to return to normal life by going fishing in Galilee, only to have the Risen Lord jolt them back to their mission (Jn 21:1–23).

Spirit-Filled Apostles

It was finally with the descent of the Holy Spirit at Pentecost that the Twelve (with Matthias then replacing Judas) became transformed men (Acts 2:1–13). On that very day, Simon Peter, who had never spoken before a crowd in his life, addressed the Israelite pilgrim people gathered in Jerusalem from many other places for the Jewish feast. He spoke with insight, courage, and even boldness as he proclaimed the truth about Jesus' identity, mission, and message. Around three thousand believed and received Baptism that day (Acts 2:14–41)!

The Acts of the Apostles uses a special word—*parresia*, in Greek—to describe the way in which the apostles began to act after the Holy Spirit had transformed them. It is hard to translate that word into English. It includes the meanings of courage, conviction, forcefulness, and even boldness. Their inspired preaching proved amazingly persuasive as they first addressed their fellow Jews and then turned to the Gentiles. After Pentecost, the apostles seemed to evidence no doubt or hesitation about their mission. They abandoned all that was familiar to them to evangelize the entire known world. What the Risen Lord had done for the two disciples on the road to Emmaus (Lk 24:13–35), they now did for the Israelite people everywhere, as they preached the fulfillment of Old Testament prophecy. When the Holy Spirit opened Gentile hearts to accept the Risen Lord and helped the apostles to realize that the Lord wanted them to expand the mission to them, they responded promptly (Acts 10:34–48) and ratified this mission at the Council of Jerusalem (Acts 15:1–29).

The New Testament writings attest to a remarkable development in the apostles' understanding of their mission. They first engaged in an inspired proclamation of the Gospel, moving from village to village, city to city! They worked extraordinary signs in support of the truth of the message. This convinced many to embrace the faith and seek Baptism.

But the apostles also faced enormous challenges. Paul alone recounted:

> Five times I have received at the hands of the Jews the forty lashes less one. Three times I have been beaten with rods; once I was stoned. Three times I have been shipwrecked; a night and a day I have been adrift at sea; on frequent journeys, in danger from rivers, danger from robbers, danger from my own people, danger from Gentiles, danger in the city, danger in the wilderness, danger at sea, danger from false brethren; in toil and hardship, through many a sleepless night, in hunger and thirst, often without food, in cold and exposure. And, apart from other things, there is the daily pressure upon me of my anxiety for all the churches. (2 Cor 11:24–28)

How many individuals have ever undergone such suffering for any cause? Yet Paul could also profess: "Indeed I count everything as loss because of the surpassing worth of knowing Christ Jesus my Lord. For his sake I have suffered the loss of all things, and count them as refuse, in order that I may gain Christ" (Phil 3:8). This fearless, undivided heart made Paul so open to God's grace that he became the model apostle for all missionaries in every age.

The Apostles as Pastors

This period of extraordinary expansion soon had to yield to the need to care for the faith communities, formed by this dramatic preaching effort. Paul himself had to wrestle with the pastoral issues that emerged in the local churches he founded. He learned of their progress and their challenges through oral or written reports to him. He, in turn, responded with oral direction or written letters. He also chose trusted collaborators, formed them in their roles, and, with the support of the local communities, ordained them with prayer and the laying on of hands. These activities were captured in his letters and especially in those letters he wrote to Timothy in Ephesus and Titus in Crete. Other apostles did likewise.

As the apostles began to lay down their lives in martyrdom for the faith, the apostolic Church began to realize that it was going to be important to provide for subsequent generations a trustworthy account of the life, Death, Resurrection, and glorification of Jesus as well as a faithful summary of his teaching. Inspired by the Holy Spirit, they began to develop succinct accounts in what the Church has called the synoptic Gospels. They also gathered from among existing apostolic letters those that the Holy Spirit wanted preserved as expressive of the Word of God in the first-century Church.

Finally, toward the end of the first century, deeper insight—that is, the fruit of reflective prayer about the mysteries of faith—became expressed especially in the Letter to the Hebrews and the Gospel according to John. These latter books of the New Testament corpus offer the fruit of decades of prayerful engagement with the life, Death, and Resurrection of the Lord and the preaching of the revelation he had revealed.

Thus, although the New Testament Scripture does not offer a systematic treatise on the gift of the priesthood, it does provide the ingredients for a deeper understanding of Jesus' own life and mission as well as the life of those he explicitly designated to serve his Church. For instance, the Letter to the Hebrews explains how Jesus revealed himself to be the one eternal priest, offering himself in the one eternal sacrifice of loving response to his Father, making possible salvation and sanctification for all who are willing to accept him. Participation in this priesthood was to be granted to all who not only believed but accepted Baptism as both Peter (1 Pet 2:4–5) and Paul (Rom 6:2–4) attested in their letters.

From among those who shared the baptismal priesthood, the Lord also chose some men to be configured with him as Head of his Body, the Church; Shepherd to his flock of disciples; and Bridegroom to his Bride, for whom he died. These men, who enjoyed various titles in the New Testament (overseers/bishops, elders/presbyters, servants/deacons, teachers), were explicitly ordained initially by one of the apostles and engaged in a threefold ministry of preaching, worship/prayer, and pastoral care to carry on the apostolic ministry originally entrusted to the Twelve.

What were the criteria looked for in those so chosen? When the apostles, under the direction of Simon Peter, first sought to choose a successor to the traitor Judas, they looked among those who had been firsthand witnesses to Jesus from his Baptism in the Jordan to his Ascension (Acts 1:21–23). Thereafter, they sought out men who had become full disciples of the Lord, evidenced integrity in living the Gospel faith and life, manifested gifts for Church leadership, and enjoyed the respect of the faithful.

So, the embrace of discipleship became decisive even if the road to discipleship was uneven. The early Church wanted men who were turning their lives over to the Lord in fulfillment of the conditions for discipleship, laid out by the Lord Jesus (Mt 16:24–28; Mk 8:34—9:1; Lk 9:23–27; 14:25–33). The Lord did not mince words when he spelled out the cost for true discipleship. In fact, the account in the fourteenth chapter of St. Luke uses a very harsh verb in seemingly requiring the disciple to "hate" even members of his own family (v. 26). The parallel passage in Matthew's Gospel helps to clarify the meaning of the Lucan hyperbole as Matthew quotes Jesus as saying: "He who loves father or mother more than me is not worthy of me" (Mt 10:37). So, the Lord lays claim to a person's *first* and *most fundamental* love. When the love of the Lord is central, then all other loves fall more easily into their proper place. Disciples are to love the Lord more than any human relationship, more than any possession, and more than life itself. This is a tall order! And it was lived out in an uneven way in subsequent eras. Reviewing this historical record can help put the present challenges to the Church due to the clergy and episcopal scandals in a helpful perspective.

Some Implications

First, this scriptural account brings home the truth that, from the beginning, the Lord chose rather ordinary men. They struggled to understand, let alone live, what Jesus was calling them to embrace. Ambition prompted two to ask for privileged places in the kingdom. The other ten then resented those two. Fear led one to deny him. Greed seduced another to betray him and then take his own life in despair. These were hardly promising apostles!

Second, these chosen men were invited to come and live with the Lord in order to grow in love of him and experience a gradual formation that would enable them both to understand and to fulfill the sacred mission that was to be entrusted to them. They were stumbling disciples who needed to *become* open to the Holy Spirit that was to be given them at Pentecost. What seemed especially to mark the life and ministry of these first apostles after Pentecost was *parresia*. These men gave every evidence of a real inner transformation, effected by the Holy Spirit, manifested in courage, conviction, and boldness in the proclamation of the Gospel. St. Paul made a special point of insisting that his spiritual son, Timothy, keep alive that gift of God within him through the laying on of his hands (2 Tim 1:6).

Third, the descent of the Holy Spirit marked a dramatically significant moment in their development and shaped their lives from that point on. The Lord Jesus had promised the Holy Spirit to his fledgling apostles at the Last Supper table. He pledged that the Holy Spirit would teach them all things and remind them of all he had revealed to them (Jn 14:26). He also prayed to the Father that the Holy Spirit would preserve them from the Evil One in the midst of all the challenges they would face in the world (Jn 17:15).

The Acts of the Apostles then offers a remarkable account of the blessed way in which the apostles, especially Peter and Paul, persevered in the face of daunting challenges in a mission that led to the planting of the faith in the then known world. Openness to the Holy Spirit, responsiveness to the Holy Spirit, and confident ministry in the Holy Spirit then characterized the extraordinary lives of the apostles. After stumbling steps in the beginning, these men became the foundation of the Church with Christ Jesus as the capstone.

Finally, even in the New Testament there is evidence of a gradual development in the way in which these apostles fulfilled their ministry. As the challenges developed, so the expression of ministry developed in organic fidelity to the original mandate. They first dispersed in a remarkable missionary effort to evangelize the then known world. They then realized they needed to provide stable leadership in the Christian communities they had established. Then, as some of them suffered martyrdom, the Holy Spirit inspired them to provide written accounts of their experience with Jesus and their early efforts to live his mission. Toward the close of the apostolic era, some of them (as reflected in the Letter to the Hebrews and the Gospel of John) engaged in sharing reflections on the deeper meaning of the Lord's life and teaching. So, development in ordained ministry in response to new challenges became normative in Church life.

In the subsequent history of the Church, God has continued to call imperfect men to serve in his name. Some became saints, others merely ordinary instruments of God's saving mission, and some, unfortunately, great sinners. This is ever the Church's story!

Lord, who have called me to be your disciple and your apostle, transform this earthen vessel by the power of your Holy Spirit, that I may embrace the priestly vocation with wisdom, courage, conviction, and boldness so that your saving mission may be realized in the lives of those you ask me to serve. Grant this in your own name. Amen.

Chapter 2

St. Ignatius of Antioch: Disciple and Martyr

The Life and Times of St. Ignatius of Antioch

St. Ignatius of Antioch offers a powerful witness to what it can mean to surrender life itself in discipleship of the Lord. Historians estimate that he was probably born about A.D. 35 and died approximately A.D. 107. So, he lived right after the Death and Resurrection of the Lord. He was a native of Antioch and became the third bishop of that local church probably in the late 90s. He succeeded Evodius, who in turn had replaced Simon Peter when the latter left Antioch to make his way to Rome.

Ignatius lived in challenging times. The first century had brought periodic persecutions of Christians in the Roman Empire, depending on the temperament and policies of each of the emperors. Trajan, who ruled from 95 to 117, sought to impose the pagan worship of the Roman gods on the entire population of the empire. Bishop Ignatius resisted the effort publicly in Antioch. When the emperor Trajan visited Antioch, he ordered Ignatius to be taken in chains to Rome to be fed to the wild beasts.

As Ignatius made his journey from port to port along the Mediterranean Sea, members of the local Christian communities did their best to offer him encouragement and support. Ignatius refused to surrender to self-pity but grew in his conviction that his sentence was actually going to enable him, in God's providence, to become more fully a disciple of the Lord in martyrdom. He was determined to offer himself first for the local church he served in Antioch but also for the ecclesial communities he met along the way.

The Letters of St. Ignatius of Antioch

During this journey, Ignatius began to write letters to each of the local churches he visited on the way to Rome. It is not known how many he may have written, but seven are extant: five addressed to ecclesial communities that offered him support; one to the Bishop of Smyrna, Polycarp; and one to the community that was to be his destination, Rome.[1]

---

[1] For a translation of Ignatius' letters, see the translation by Gerald Walsh in *The Fathers of the Church*, trans. Francis X. Glimm, Joseph M.-F. Marique, S.J., and Gerald Walsh (New York: Cima Publishing, 1947). Subsequent citations refer to this translation.

In the five letters written to the communities he had met along the way, Ignatius provided the earliest historical evidence that, by the end of the first century, the local churches had already in place bishops as successors of the apostles, presbyters as their chief collaborators, and deacons offering service to those in need. Ignatius offered repeated exhortations to unity in faith and gospel living in communion with the local bishop. He cautioned against compromising the faith by yielding to the Docetists, who denied the real humanity of Christ, or compromising religious practice by being misled by Judaizers, who wanted to impose Jewish ritual practices on Gentile Christians. In his *Letter to Polycarp*, Ignatius urged courage in the face of the tumultuous times, fidelity in teaching, and perseverance in both pastoral care of the faithful and his own life of prayer and virtue.

It is in Ignatius' *Letter to the Romans* that he made an impassioned appeal not to derail his death sentence by any misguided attempts to intervene. He likened his destiny to the Eucharistic sacrifice of the Lord: "I am God's wheat; I am ground by the teeth of the wild beasts that I may end as the pure bread of Christ."[2]

Ignatius offered in his letters a succinct expression of the early Christian *kerygma*. He not only preached but lived the biblical worldview. Life in this world is a pilgrimage toward another life, profoundly real and ultimately more important than anything this world offers. During his life in this world, the Son of God revealed the face of the Father. The bishop is to be so united with Christ that he becomes "theophorus", a name he used for himself; that is, he is to "bear God". The faithful experience communion with God through their ecclesial communion

[2] *Letter to the Romans* 4.

with their bishop.[3] The Eucharist is the greatest expression of this saving and sanctifying communion with Christ.[4] The goal of the Christian life is salvation and the destiny of each Christian is the life to come.[5]

Ignatius interpreted life's journey in this world as a pilgrimage in discipleship.[6] It involves an engagement of both body and soul in living the life of the Spirit. He was eager to complete his discipleship in martyrdom as the ultimate expression of pastoral love, a complete self-gift to God for the Church.[7]

As Ignatius addressed the need to both laity and priests to live in conformity with the Gospel, he lifted up communion with the Lord through ecclesial communion with their bishops as foundational. He used the image of a choir under the guidance of a director.[8] He urged a truly spiritual communion with their bishop that goes beyond human considerations.[9] He encouraged union in belief[10] and in conscience.[11]

Ignatius urged the ordained to give of themselves in pastoral charity.[12] This charity, rooted in true faith,[13] needs self-discipline in practice[14] and expresses itself in care for the

---

[3] *Letter to the Ephesians* 1, 4, 5, 20; *Letter to the Magnesians* 1–4, 7; *Letter to the Trallians* 1–3, 7, 13; *Letter to the Philadelphians* 2, 4, 7; *Letter to the Smyrnaeans* 8; *Letter to Polycarp* 1.

[4] *Letter to the Romans* 4, 7; *Letter to the Philadelphians* 4; *Letter to the Smyrnaeans* 7.

[5] *Letter to the Ephesians* 11; *Letter to the Romans* 6.

[6] *Letter to the Ephesians* 3; *Letter to the Magnesians* 14.

[7] *Letter to the Romans* 2–8; *Letter to the Ephesians* 8, 18, 21; *Letter to Polycarp* 6.

[8] *Letter to the Ephesians* 4.

[9] Ibid., 5.

[10] *Letter to the Ephesians* 7, 9, 18; *Letter to Polycarp* 3.

[11] *Letter to the Magnesians* 7.

[12] *Letter to Polycarp* 1.

[13] Ibid., 1, 3.

[14] Ibid., 1, 2.

sick and needy.[15] The bishop is to care that the vocations of marriage, celibacy, and Holy Orders are lived faithfully.[16]

Thus, Ignatius embraced a red (bloody) martyrdom for himself, even as he encouraged a white (unbloody) martyrdom for those called to ordained ministry in the local ecclesial communities. Both he regarded as expressions of total self-gift in discipleship of the Lord.

Some Implications

St. Ignatius of Antioch offers an insight into the priesthood that provides further perspective on the living of the priesthood: the priest is called to be a priest-victim, like the Lord; this priest-victimhood needs to be deepened gradually in the celebration of Christ's priestly victimhood in the Eucharist. It is impossible to read the testimony of Ignatius of Antioch without sensing the intensity and generosity of spirit that shaped his life. He wanted to be as closely identified as possible with the self-emptying and self-gift that St. Paul described as lived by the Lord Jesus (Phil 1:5–11). Ignatius wanted to be one with Christ as priest and victim. He wanted to express it by giving up his own body and pouring out his blood as did the Lord. He provided testimony in life and death to the saving and sanctifying mission of the Lord.

So, Ignatius encouraged bishops and priests to recognize that there is a profound relationship between the way the Lord Jesus lived his priesthood and the way that the ordained are to live out their priesthood. Christ had superseded all previous expressions of sacrifice by offering

[15] Ibid., 1.
[16] Ibid., 5.

himself as the victim. If any priest is to realize the gift granted in his ordination, he has to appreciate that he, too, is called to be both priest and victim in his own life. When he proclaims in Christ's name, "This is my Body, which will be given up for you"; "this is the chalice of my Blood, ... which will be poured out for you and for many for the forgiveness of sins," he is called to unite his own body and blood in that sacrifice. Ignatius witnessed to that powerfully in his life and in his sacrificial death. During this period of persistent persecution, a few bishops and priests faltered. Some handed over scriptural texts and liturgical articles that the persecutors were demanding. Some even pretended to offer pagan worship to save their own lives. But most offered a powerful witness to faith and fortitude, thus inspiring the laity to persevere.

Lord, who in the Eucharist offer your own Body and Blood anew in sacrament, help me, like St. Ignatius of Antioch, to offer my body and blood with you to the Father for the sake of the people you call me to serve. Give me the grace to be faithful in the face of resistance or opposition. Enable me to persevere unto death in giving witness to you. All this I pray in your own name. Amen.

Chapter 3

St. John Chrysostom:
Engagement in the Spiritual Struggle

The World of St. John Chrysostom

The early fourth century ushered in a new era for the Church. Although the prospect of persecution dominated a good bit of the Church's experience during the first three centuries, the Edict of Milan in 312 provided religious freedom for Christians. Emperor Constantine attributed his victory at the Milvian Bridge to Christ's intervention, because a cross in the sky had marked the turning point in the battle. With the encouragement of his saintly mother, Helena, he declared an end to the Roman Empire's hostility to Christianity.

As the Church moved from an underground (catacomb) existence to life in the mainstream, Christians enjoyed the freedom to build churches and live Christian life in public. But, without the threat of imprisonment or death, Christians became more lax in their living of the faith. Many began to make accommodations to the wider world culture. Thus, mediocrity and spiritual sloth became more pervasive.

In this atmosphere, some Christians sought to explore more explicitly what it might mean to live a more radical Gospel life in the world. Some moved into the desert to explore the reality of God and the truth about themselves, others, the world, and the demonic. While a few hardy souls made a lifelong commitment to this way of life, others made their way for shorter periods. These latter often sought spiritual inspiration or guidance from those who had persevered in eremitical life. In these new circumstances, engagement in the explicitly spiritual struggle of conversion of life, growth in prayer, and progress in virtue supplanted the willingness to accept martyrdom as the privileged expression of Gospel discipleship.

The Life of St. John Chrysostom

This was the environment in which John Chrysostom lived. He, like Ignatius, was born in Antioch, in 345. Although there were brief periods of persecution of faithful Christians in Antioch under Emperor Julian the Apostate (361–363) and the Arian emperor Valens (365–376), Antioch had become a city where Christians held the emerging eremetical and coenobitical life in high esteem.

John benefitted by the best in education available at that time in philosophy, rhetoric, and Sacred Scripture. But his heart hungered for a fuller living of Gospel discipleship.

His widowed mother had sacrificed greatly to provide this exceptional education. When she learned that John was planning to move into eremetical life, she intervened and begged him to recognize his duty toward her after all the sacrifices she had made for him. So he remained at home, taught school, and supported her for almost a decade to provide for her before taking the steps to pursue his sense of God's call.

Meanwhile John's very close friend Basil had already embarked on the eremetical life. The Bishop of Antioch recognized the unusual integrity and the rich gifts that both John and Basil manifested. He urged both of them to be open to a call to the priesthood. Neither was inclined. But John pretended to accept in order to encourage Basil to do so. Basil then accepted ordination, unaware that John had reneged.

After John had spent six years in the desert, he returned to Antioch and accepted the vocational call to priesthood. Eventually, he was to become Archbishop of Constantinople. Shortly after his ordination to the priesthood, he composed a treatise on the priesthood that had the dual purpose of repairing his relationship with his esteemed Basil (then the Bishop of Caesarea) and sharing the fruit of his own reflections on the awesome call to priestly life and ministry. This treatise provides a profound insight into the nature of the spiritual struggle that a good priest needs to be willing to embrace if he is really going to help those entrusted to his care to realize their God-given vocation as well.

Treatise on the Priesthood

John Chrysostom had come to appreciate that Christian discipleship involved a spiritual struggle. An underlying theme in Sacred Scripture is the account of a spiritual war that Satan, the fallen and desperate Lucifer, has waged against God for the souls of men. The third chapter in the Book of Genesis recounts the beginning of that war with the seduction of Adam and Eve. The twelfth chapter of the Book of Revelation presents a vision of the ultimate triumph over Satan by Michael the Archangel. The whole biblical narrative records repeated skirmishes in the history of salvation. During his public ministry, Jesus engaged in some dramatic episodes in which he exercised divine power over the diabolical efforts of countless demons. It was in his Resurrection and Ascension that the Lord Jesus revealed his definitive victory over the hour of darkness and the power of evil and death.

Since this biblical understanding of the deeper struggles people face in life is so important, John Chrysostom was convinced that true disciples of the Lord needed to engage in this spiritual effort. This is what led him into the desert initially. This is what made him also apprehensive about answering the call to ordination. For him, the monastic vocation was easier to embrace because it introduced so many safeguards to help the monk focus on this struggle. The priestly vocation posed more challenges because the ordained were called to live in the world, while not succumbing to the temptations of the world. They not only had to be engaged in the spiritual battle themselves but had to try to help the faithful take this struggle seriously as well.[1]

This realization led Chrysostom to be convinced that the priest was the *crucible* in which the struggle for the salvation and sanctification of souls had to take place. If the

[1] John Chrysostom, *The Priesthood* VI, 2, 4, 6 (Crestwood, NY: St. Vladimir's Seminary Press, 1996).

priest is to fulfill this challenging role, he must be willing
to make the spiritual struggle central in his own life so that
he can help others as well.

Chrysostom gave special attention to the motive appropriate for saying yes to a priestly vocation: the salvation and
sanctification of others. He considered unacceptable any
desire for recognition, status, or power.[2] He also criticized
any ambition in this regard.[3] Thus, Chrysostom urged
discernment lest the desire for power, glory, or authority
over others replace the desire to work for the salvation and
sanctification of souls.

Chrysostom also proposed a time of preparation that
focused on the development of personal virtue so that the
priest would eventually acquire pastoral virtue. This preparation was not to address so much the physical austerities
proper to the life of a monk but the inner strength of character that would enable him to handle the seductions of
the world, opposition to sound teaching, and the ordinary
trials of offering pastoral care.

This means that the priest has to take seriously the
Christian struggle with the capital sins, the fundamental
inclinations to sin in our fallen human nature. Hence,
pride or vainglory needs to yield to humility. Chrysostom
found this a particular challenge in preaching because
of his special gift of eloquence.[4] The tendency to greed
requires the development of not only detachment regarding worldly benefits[5] but also a concrete concern for the
needs of the poor.[6] An irascible temperament undermines

[2] Ibid., III, 3–4, 9, 15.
[3] Ibid., III, 10–11.
[4] Ibid., III, 9.
[5] Ibid., III, 11, 16.
[6] Ibid., III, 6.

pastoral charity.[7] So the priest needs to develop gentleness
in the correction of others.[8] Lust also subverts the true
love of charity—hence the need for chastity[9] and discernment in all pastoral relationships embraced in ministry.[10]
Sobriety and moderation should replace gluttony so that
a disciplined way of life gives credibility to the preaching
of the Gospel message.[11] Being at home in one's own
identity and mission should replace any envy or jealousy
about the lives others are living.[12] Finally, spiritual initiative or zeal needs to counteract any mediocrity or sloth in
the fulfillment of the priestly vocation.[13]

In his homilies on marriage and family life, St. John
Chrysostom also offered to priests an example of good
pastoral insight and care for the marital vocation.
Although some commentators focus on earlier writing
wherein Chrysostom tried to dissuade a brother monk
from abandoning his vocation by presenting marriage for
him in negative terms, his later homilies on St. Paul's
letters to the Colossians and Ephesians present a powerful
invitation to married couples to realize the exalted dignity and holiness to which they are called. They offer a
mature expression of the way ordained priesthood serves
the lay priesthood.[14]

[7] Ibid., III, 14.
[8] Ibid., II, 2.
[9] Ibid., III, 4.
[10] Ibid., III, 17.
[11] Ibid., III, 12–13, 15.
[12] Ibid., III, 13; IV, 4.
[13] Ibid., VI, 3.
[14] See Mike Aquilina, "Chrysostom and the Mysteries of Marriage", *Mike
Aquilina: The Fathers of the Church* (Mike Aquilina's website), April 4, 2008,
https://fathersofthechurch.com/2008/04/04/chrysostom-and-the-mysteries
-of-marriage/.

Some Implications

St. John Chrysostom makes a significant contribution to the understanding of priestly life and ministry in focusing first on the right motive for accepting ordination and second on the spiritual struggle that the priest needs to embrace in order to bring the Gospel alive.

In rejecting any desire for recognition, status, comfort, or power, Chrysostom highlighted the only motive worthy of the priestly vocation: the salvation and sanctification of others. God can use less perfect motivation to attract potential candidates at first. But if the motivation is not purified and refined, if the salvation and sanctification of others do not supersede and replace earlier, less appropriate motives, then it is better to help candidates realize the priestly vocation is not theirs. Priesthood is not a career, but a sacred vocation for others.

St. John Chrysostom also rightly urged serious attention to the development of the virtues made possible by faithful engagement in the spiritual struggle. He never claimed proficiency in these virtues in his own life. In fact, he shared the challenges he himself experienced in trying to live them. His hope was that ongoing attention to these struggles on the part of a priest would enable the priest to live his own life call faithfully and would keep alive the central challenge of helping the faithful reach their ultimate goal in life. For unless the priest is focused on this, it will be difficult for the faithful to recognize the centrality of this struggle in their own lives. Discipleship of the Lord, then, need not involve a red martyrdom. It may be a white martyrdom in service to the Lord. In fact, it involved just that for John Chrysostom, for he was exiled by Queen Eudoxia for his challenges to her way of life, and then died alone and abandoned in Comana, Pontus, in 407.

Time and again in the history of the Church, priests are going to struggle with the temptation to make a false accommodation to the life of the world. There is a significant difference between Gospel life and worldly life. The ordained priest receives the Gospel in trust. He is to listen attentively to the Word of God, ponder its meaning, live it in practice, and preach it to the faithful. In doing so, he will inevitably find resistance in the world. The easier approach will always be to adjust the Gospel message so as to make it more acceptable to a fallen world. If he does this, he will begin to water down the challenging dimensions of that message in his own life and lead those entrusted to his care to do the same. But if he truly enters into the struggle envisioned by that message, for the sake of loving the world in the way the Lord loves the world, he will become a witness to life-giving truth. He will also help others to do the same.

Lord Jesus, who have called me to enter into discipleship, involving conversion of life and growth in virtue, help me, like St. John Chrysostom, to embrace that spiritual struggle generously and faithfully so that I may live in the world, but not of the world, and may serve the salvation and sanctification of others by inspiring them to become your disciples as well. Grant this in your own name. Amen.

Chapter 4

St. Augustine:
City of God or City of Man?

The Life of St. Augustine of Hippo

As St. John Chrysostom was serving as Patriarchal Archbishop of Constantinople, Augustine was finding his
way into the Church and then ordination as a priest.
Chrysostom emerged from the Church of the Christian
East; Augustine from the Christian West. Augustine was
born in Tagaste, North Africa, in 354 to a saintly mother
and a pagan father. His mother wanted him to accept Baptism and live a responsible Christian life. His father, rather
authoritarian and distant, wanted him to be a successful
man of the world. When his father had set aside enough

money, he sent Augustine to Carthage to benefit by the advanced schooling in rhetoric available there.

When Augustine arrived in Carthage, he immersed himself in university life. He excelled in his studies. He not only plunged into the reading of the great classical literature, but he also explored philosophical writings. At the end of his first year in Carthage, his father, Patricius, died unexpectedly. Augustine had never really resolved his turbulent relationship with his father. This sudden loss set Augustine adrift. He became promiscuous and then settled into a live-in relationship with a young woman with whom he fathered a son.

Augustine's philosophical curiosity was piqued by his reading of Cicero's *Hortensius*. But he was not sure where to seek the truth. He briefly revisited the Bible, to which his mother had introduced him. The Latin translation available was unbelievably bad. The biblical narrative did not engage him. Then some of his fellow students suggested that he explore Manichaeism. Those who were devotees seemed to exude an air of intellectual superiority and confidence. Augustine was to stay with them for nine years, including years of teaching after concluding his university studies. Eventually he met one of their highly regarded teachers, Faustus, whom he discovered to be a fraud. This disillusioned him and led him to abandon Manichaeism and his teaching role in Carthage to pursue a new life across the Mediterranean Sea in Rome.

The Roman chapter in Augustine's life was not a happy one. The students he was teaching seemed more interested in learning rhetoric in order to succeed in life than in reading classical literature in search of truth—and a number of them failed miserably in paying their bills. He himself was becoming a skeptic as he lost confidence in being able to reach objective truth about the really significant issues:

the meaning of life and death, the mystery of evil, and the purpose of daily existence.

Augustine decided to join some friends in Cassiciacum near Lake Como. They had begun to form a small group exploring philosophical issues in a serious and disciplined way. Some of them introduced him to Neoplatonism, a philosophy that adapted Platonic thought to Christianity. One invited him to travel with him to Milan to hear Bishop Ambrose preach at the cathedral. He had never heard anyone before preach with such eloquence, insight, and conviction about the Christian faith. Ambrose's ability to break open Sacred Scripture with wisdom and persuasiveness attracted Augustine. Augustine eventually met with Bishop Ambrose and then became a catechumen in preparation for Baptism the following Easter. He separated from his live-in companion, who then returned to Carthage.

Monica, Augustine's mother, had followed him to Rome and then to Milan. She prayed and sacrificed that he might receive the grace of Christian faith. When Augustine accepted the waters of Baptism, she could not contain herself with joy. She decided then to return to Africa, where she wanted to complete her earthly pilgrimage. Augustine would not let her go alone and, while they were in Ostia, awaiting passage on a ship, Monica took ill. Augustine confided to her that he might give up his dream of a life of philosophical writing and teaching in order to present himself as a candidate for the priesthood. Monica was convinced her mission in life was complete. She died in Ostia before they ever set sail for Africa.

Augustine returned to his native land and presented himself as a candidate for ordination. His extensive studies meant that he needed no further academic work, merely an apprenticeship. His son had become a companion in the communal life that Augustine was living with others who wanted to support one another in Christian discipleship. Unfortunately, he died young a few years after Augustine's arrival in Africa. After ordination, Augustine served as a priest only a few years when it became clear that he had remarkable gifts for leadership. He was appointed Coadjutor Bishop of Hippo and became the Ordinary in a very short time.

Augustine's Confessions

As Augustine assumed the role as Bishop of Hippo, he was painfully aware of the meandering journey that had marked his life. He wanted to be transparent with the people he had been asked to serve. This is what prompted his writing the *Confessions* as an extended expression of prayer directed to God. Although the realization dawned on him only after a circuitous journey, he wrote in the very first chapter, "Our hearts are made for you, O God, and they will not rest until they rest in you."[1] He then recounted in far greater detail the journey just described above. He prayed in thanksgiving after recounting his conversion in Book X of his *Confessions*: "Late have I loved you, Beauty so ancient and so new!"[2]

On the first anniversary of his ordination, Augustine was to acknowledge that his journey toward Baptism was far more significant than his call to become a bishop. "For you I am a bishop, with you, after all, I am a Christian. The first is the name of an office undertaken, the second a name of grace; that one means danger, this one salvation."[3]

[1] Augustine, *Confessions* I, 1, trans. John Ryan (New York: Doubleday Image, 1960).

[2] Ibid., X, 27.

[3] Augustine, *Sermon* 340, 1, trans. Edmund Hill, ed. John Rotelle (Hyde Park, NY: New City Press, 1994).

Augustine's personal spiritual journey offers so much to those who engage in a spiritual search in every age. He learned early that things were not always what they seemed to be.[4] It had not been easy for him to name what was sinful to be sin, such as pride.[5] In his journey to conversion, he found himself praying for chastity, "but not yet".[6] He had to come to grips with spiritual sin as even more challenging than carnal sin.[7] He struggled to appreciate that real freedom is interior and related to a greater capacity to choose the good.[8] Bishop Ambrose helped him realize that the faith he had rejected was a counterfeit expression of true Christian faith. How many struggle with these very same issues today!

The City of God

Probably the most significant struggle for Augustine he addressed in his book *The City of God*.[9] This book was in part a philosophy of history. He wanted to address the charge that the collapse of the Roman Empire was due to Christianity. In it he grappled with the most fundamental issue of human life. He came to realize that individuals have to make a fundamental choice in life. Are they going to choose God rather than anyone or anything else in the world? Or are they going to choose self? While this is always a personal decision, it has profound implications for the way people live with others. The more people are

[4] *Confessions* V; VI, 3–4.
[5] Ibid., VIII, 3, 21; X, 29–43.
[6] Ibid., VIII, 7.
[7] Ibid., VI, 6.
[8] Ibid., VII, 18; VIII, 12; IX, 1.
[9] Augustine, *The City of God*, trans. Gerald Walsh and Grace Monahan (New York: Fathers of the Church, 1952), vols. 8, 14, 24.

living for God, the more they realize the *city of God* even on earth. The more people are living for themselves, the more they foster the *city of man* with all its attendant problems. Augustine had to face this radically in his own life. The choice for God over self came to define Christian discipleship for him.

Augustine's Sermons on the Priesthood

Augustine had experienced the years he spent in Cassiciacum as personally deeply enriching. He was strongly attracted to the intellectual life and the companionship of like-minded philosophers. But he sensed God was calling him to relinquish his personal dream in favor of a public gift of himself to the Church. This was not an easy choice to make. But once made, Augustine found a new freedom as he channeled his remarkable gifts in service to the Church. For him, ordination meant the embrace of an ecclesial social office that required the full-time, all-absorbing gift of himself to God for the Lord's saving mission in the Church. In his homily on the anniversary of his ordination, he expressed the awesome responsibilities of his role as a bishop in this way: "The turbulent have to be corrected, the faint-hearted cheered up, the weak supported; the Gospel's opponents need to be refuted, its insidious enemies guarded against; the unlearned need to be taught, the indolent stirred up, the argumentative checked; the proud need to be put in their place, the desperate set on their feet, those engaged in quarrels reconciled; the needy have to be helped, the oppressed to be liberated, the good to be given your backing, the bad to be tolerated; all must be loved."[10]

---

[10] *Sermon* 340, 3.

Augustine wanted the ordained to realize that they were living instruments in God's hands. To emphasize this, he referred to the scriptural images contained in the Lord's parables: the innkeeper in service to the Good Samaritan, the planter or the overseer in service to the owner of the field or vineyard, the servant in service to the head of the household. In each of these parables, the cited figure served as a steward for someone more important than himself. He was to treat his responsibilities as a sacred trust. Priests cannot expect to be in charge of their own lives. For Augustine, the ordained were ministers of the *mystery*. This *mystery* was God's saving presence and action. The *mystery* becomes especially expressed in the sacramental life of the Church.

Augustine also gave great significance to faithful ministry to the Word of God. He compared the Word of God to food, bread, light, water, medicine, and seed for souls. He wanted the priest to reverence the Word and minister to it with care. He urged the preacher to engage in serious prayer and study, but always to respect the internal Word that Christ wanted to stir in the heart of the hearers.[11] Hence, he urged the preacher to cultivate in his heart the desire to preach in such a way that God's Word, not his own word, is heard. Preaching fruitfully depends more on the Master's Word within than the personal rhetoric of the preacher.

As Bishop of Hippo, Augustine participated in the Church's condemnation of Donatism. Donatus had claimed that those priests and bishops who failed to profess the faith or who handed over the Scriptures during the persecutions did not then exercise the Sacrament of Holy Orders validly, even after repentance. He taught that such men, after returning to the faith, needed to be reordained. He also

[11] Ibid., 46, 33–35.

thought that those who had received sacraments from them did not receive valid sacraments. Donatists, followers of Donatus, then taught that any seriously sinful priests or bishops did not exercise valid ministry. Augustine took a strong position against Donatism, arguing persuasively that God continued to offer grace through the sacraments celebrated by a sinful priest or bishop for the sake of the faithful. He in no way countenanced the sins of such unfaithful shepherds, but distinguished God's fidelity in offering the grace to recipients from the sacrilegious sinfulness of those celebrating the sacraments under these circumstances. Augustine's teaching was ratified as the teaching of the Church in the Council of Carthage and was later reaffirmed in the Council of Trent. He urged the faithful not to leave the Church because of bad pastors.[12] This exhortation has powerful ramifications for today!

Some Implications

St. Augustine offers real encouragement to those who struggle to develop the virtues important for priestly life. His amazing intellect inclined him to arrogance and pride. His struggle with human sexuality kept the fires of lust burning within him. But inspired preaching and the witness of men he respected led him to his knees in conversion and the embrace of a graced life.

Augustine's special contribution to priestly life and ministry was to highlight movement from self-serving love to self-giving love. For him, the ascetism appropriate for the priest and bishop focused on the development of those virtues that enable him to engage in self-giving service of the Lord in the Church. He learned from his own experience

---

[12] Ibid., 46, 28–29.

that being available to God was more important than fulfilling his own dreams. Obedience to God's will has to
supersede personal preference. Self-gift has to replace selfish preoccupation.[13] Humility and living the truth make
this more possible.[14] Most of all, the spirit of *prodesse*
needs to replace the attitude of *praesse*.[15] This means the
attitude of "service to" has to replace "presiding over"
those entrusted in pastoral care.

Augustine, of course, eventually became recognized as a
saint. His uneven journey has to be a source of consolation
and reassurance for priests who become painfully aware of
the truth of St. Paul's words: "But we have this treasure
in earthen vessels, to show that the transcendent power
belongs to God and not to us" (2 Cor 4:7). But Augustine
also challenged priests to recognize that a conscious decision to turn their lives over to the Lord needs to shape their
self-gift and constantly needs to be renewed and deepened.
Otherwise priests can succumb to the self-serving practices
that Augustine so explicitly condemned.[16] Shepherds are
to feed the flock, not themselves—to seek the good of
souls, not clerical privilege and special treatment. For the
ordained, true discipleship of the Lord involves an ever
fuller self-gift to the Lord for the salvation of others.

*Lord Jesus, who have called me to make a sacrificial gift of myself
and to resist selfish behavior in order to serve your Church, help
me through the intercession of St. Augustine to realize that gift
in my own life and to assist others to choose you above all else in
their lives. Grant this in your own name. Amen.*

[13] Ibid., 46, 7–9.
[14] Ibid., 46, 7–9.
[15] Ibid., 46, 2.
[16] Ibid., 46, 5–22.

Chapter 5

St. Gregory: The Art of Arts

St. Gregory and His Times

Two centuries later another remarkable man contributed
to an appreciation of the kind of discipleship needed in
ordained priesthood. Gregory was born in Rome in 540
at a time when numerous Germanic tribes were invading
the territories that once were part of the Roman Empire.
These less civilized people often terrorized the residents.
First it was the Goths in the 40s, then the Franks in the
50s and the Lombards in the 60s. With the old order of
the empire crumbling, people scrambled to develop a new
way of providing law, order, and safety. By this time, the
Church had established herself as the most trusted entity
to help stabilize and normalize ordinary life. In this situation, local leaders often emerged to supplant appointees

of the emperor. Sometimes bishops, abbots, and pastors accepted an expanding role in the temporal order. This is how feudalism emerged as people looked to lords to provide the social stability that had been lost. This is also how the church and state became closely intertwined in the early Middle Ages.

In this atmosphere, Gregory grew up in Rome. He came from a family of wealth and received an education to prepare him for public service. In 570 he became the Prefect of Rome.

But Gregory experienced an inner call to a deeper life. When his father died in 575, Gregory decided to turn the home he inherited into a monastery. It is not clear how much he initially knew of Benedict's initiatives in Subiaco and Monte Cassino. But he experienced a very similar desire to gather a group of like-minded men to support one another in living a more radical evangelical life in a time that was not often that friendly to Gospel values. Later on, Gregory wrote an account of Benedict's life and work.

Gregory's way of life and his obvious gifts for leadership drew the attention of Pope Benedict I. He invited Gregory to consider ordination to the priesthood. Gregory was reluctant, but he did accept the order of deacon. Pope Pelagius II then sent him to Byzantium as a Papal Legate to help ease the increasing tensions between the Church of the Christian East and the Church of the Christian West. Gregory brought his fledgling monastic community with him. His efforts in Byzantium seemed to bear good fruit. So, Pope Pelagius II called him back to Rome as a personal consultor. When Pelagius died in 590, the College of Cardinals elected Gregory to serve as pope even though he was still just a deacon. He was ordained both priest and bishop in order to exercise the papacy as Bishop of Rome.

As pope, Gregory helped the people recover from a devastating flood of the Tiber River and successfully protected Rome from a second invasion of the Lombard tribe by negotiating a peace treaty. As a result, the people turned to Gregory as their protector and asked him to assume temporal responsibilities as well. This sowed the seeds for what eventually were to be called the Papal States.

But Gregory's heart was not in this civic role. He wanted to promote the spiritual renewal of the Church by bringing to the Church at large some of the teaching and the practices he had learned through his experiment with monastic living and his experience in Byzantium. Thus, he took advantage of his position to preach regularly on the Gospel way of life. He oversaw liturgical reform culminating in the development of the Gregorian Sacramentary. He fostered a much more cooperative relationship with the Patriarch of Constantinople. While standing for Roman primacy, he referred to himself as *Servus Servorum Dei* (the Servant of the Servants of God).

Pastoral Care

Gregory recognized that the renewal of the Church was going to be most profoundly promoted if this renewal took place in the life and ministry of priests. Hence, he wrote his *Pastoral Care* as a treatise on spiritual formation for priests.[1] Over succeeding generations, this insightful teaching reached more and more priests. Bishop Leander of Seville circulated it in Spain. Augustine of Canterbury,

---

[1] Gregory the Great, *Pastoral Care*, trans. Henry Davis, in *Ancient Christian Writers*, ed. Johannes Quasten and Joseph Plumpe (Westminster, MD: Newman Press, 1955).

a disciple of Gregory in the monastery he established in his home, brought it to England. Columban brought it to Ireland. Anastasius translated it into Greek so that it could be a leaven for renewal in the Christian East. A few centuries later, this book became an instrument of priestly renewal during the Carolingian Reform.

In *Pastoral Care*, Gregory addressed several topics in four "books": first, the motive and dispositions important for approaching the priestly vocation; second, the virtues needed to live priestly life well; third, the spiritual approach to priestly pastoral ministry; lastly, the ongoing need for self-examination in the lives of priests.

Gregory's teaching was rooted in Sacred Scripture. Since the goal of Christian life is salvation and holiness of life, the priest is called to embrace the *art of arts*,[2] the pastoral art of leading souls to God and his saving/sanctifying grace. In order to be a good priest, he must be a master of spiritual discernment.[3] He has a very real challenge to keep focused on not what pleases people but what ought to please them.[4] Rather than focus first on the spiritual exercises that a priest needs to incorporate into his life, Gregory focused on the responsibilities and demands involved in that ministry to identify the virtues and practices needed to fulfill his duties well.

First, Gregory addressed the proper motivation for priesthood. The primary motive has to be the desire to help others experience salvation and sanctification.[5] If that motive is wanting, if there is no life of prayer, if there is no real engagement with conversion of life, if an undisciplined lust has control of the heart, or if covetousness

[2] Ibid., I, 1.
[3] Ibid., II, 9.
[4] Ibid., II, 8.
[5] Ibid., II, 7.

rules the soul, then he should not consider himself a candidate for ordination.[6] Gregory placed special emphasis on covetousness, because it expresses a disordered desire for comfort in this world at the expense of the next. This disposition then leads a priest to want to use the priesthood for his own worldly purpose rather than serve the eternal destiny of the people he is called to save. He also considered it seriously wrong to run away from the challenges of a vocation, if God has truly given the gifts for it.[7] It is appropriate to turn away from such a vocation, if in genuine humility and knowledge of self he recognizes that the gifts are not there.[8] But a man should not be afraid of generous self-gift, if God is truly calling.

In addressing the virtues that ought to mark the life of a priest in the second book, Gregory, like John Chrysostom, hoped that the priest should have taken seriously the ascetical effort needed to ensure that the capital vices do not dominate his life.[9] Only if he has engaged in that struggle will he be able to live with a less divided heart,[10] maintain a reflective silence,[11] be profitable in speech,[12] and compassionate toward those he serves.[13]

By far the largest section of Gregory's treatise (the third book) focuses on the spirituality of pastoral care. To do this well, the priest must be a man of spiritual discernment. Gregory maintained that the Gospel teaching was the same for all, but people face diverse challenges in their lives in

[6] Ibid., I, 11.
[7] Ibid., I, 5.
[8] Ibid., I, 6.
[9] Ibid., II, 9.
[10] Ibid., II, 2.
[11] Ibid., II, 4.
[12] Ibid.
[13] Ibid., II, 5.

their efforts to live that teaching.[14] For instance, the poor
need to be encouraged while being kept from coveting
what the rich possess. The rich need to be urged not to
become proud and self-sufficient while being challenged
to help the needy.[15] The impudent need a harsh rebuke.
The timid need to be corrected more indirectly.[16] Gregory
went on to identify almost forty situations that the priest
may encounter and contrasted the approaches that should
be taken, dependent on the temperament and tendencies
present in each. Each approach provided a concrete example of how to offer counsel, not pandering to what people
would have liked to hear, but giving them what they
needed to hear. He concluded this section with the admo-
nition that the priest needs to preach not only in word but
in the way he lives his life.[17]

Finally, Gregory concluded his treatise in the fourth
book by urging the priest to engage in ongoing self-
examination about all the above, lest he become arrogant
or lose a sense of reverence for the sacred dimension of the
service he is being asked to render.[18]

Some Implications

St. Gregory was a master of spiritual discernment in pastoral ministry. He wanted priests to be faithful to the
Gospel teaching handed on to them, while developing
a keen appreciation of the pastoral needs of the people.
He considered it to be the greatest of arts to relate God's

[14] Ibid., III, 1.
[15] Ibid., III, 2.
[16] Ibid., III, 7.
[17] Ibid., III, 40.
[18] Ibid., IV.

revelation and the demands of the Gospel to people coming from varied backgrounds and experiencing diverse challenges.

Unfortunately, Pope Gregory set an unhappy precedent in accepting civic responsibilities along with his ecclesial ministry. This opened up the possibility for bishops, abbots, and even some pastors to do the same. This feudal practice compromised the Church's unique mission and ministry. Although Gregory did it reluctantly, others began to enjoy their increased stature and power. This gradually led to the blurring of their distinctive role and sometimes to the corruption of their way of life, as will be described in the following chapter.

Gregory had feared that this might happen. He tried to clarify what was truly proper to priestly ministry in his *Pastoral Care*. In it he outlined an approach to priestly life and ministry, marked by both personal and pastoral discernment about what God was asking of him. This approach was aimed at ensuring that the priest was living in communion with the Lord and under the inspiration of the Holy Spirit. While John Chrysostom moved from the ascetical struggle to pastoral engagement, Gregory moved from the demands of pastoral ministry to the ascetical effort it required.

It is also important to note that Gregory enunciated the basic principles for a sound inculturation of the Gospel. In his teaching on the importance for the good pastor to discern what needs to be strengthened and what should be resisted in the pastoral care of individual persons, he laid the groundwork for a similar discernment in the evangelization of cultures. Pastoral love embraces what is compatible and resists what is inimical to the Gospel. This has become more important to appreciate as the culture has become less Christian and more secular.

Lord Jesus, who has called me to a careful spiritual discernment both in living out my own life of discipleship and in serving the call to discipleship of your people, teach me both how to be true to your teaching and to accompany your people in their response to you. Grant this in your own name. Amen.

Chapter 6

St. Bernard of Clairvaux: Spiritual Fatherhood

The Feudal Culture

Between Gregory and Bernard there was a span of over five hundred years. People who lived in those centuries experienced the expansion of a Catholic world. Augustine of Canterbury had evangelized England; Boniface, Germany; Ansgar, the northern countries in the Scandinavian Peninsula; Cyril and Methodius, the Slavic countries.

This expanding Catholic world became deeply immersed in civic life through the feudal social structure that had spread throughout the European continent. Bishops, pastors, and abbots often became feudal lords. As such they were expected to provide not only Church leadership but also the protections and services associated with temporal rule. This brought with it serious challenges. There were frequent tensions between the sacral and secular responsibilities. In this arrangement, the spiritual mission of the Church often became compromised. Lay investiture, a practice of lay temporal lords influencing or deciding who would become bishops, became a significant challenge for the freedom and independence of the Church. With this, not only mediocrity but moral corruption invaded Church life.

A number of reform efforts tried to address this. Some of these reformers tackled the needed renewal with passion and zeal, but became heretical, such as the Waldensians and Albigensians. Others remained faithful and constructive such as St. Peter Damian. He tried to root out sexual moral decadence and financial corruption in the clergy. He was often very explicit and direct in condemning both heterosexual and homosexual immorality among the clergy. Both popes Nicholas II and Gregory VII relied on the good preaching, teaching, and writing of Peter Damian in their efforts to promote ecclesial reform. St. Bruno founded the Carthusians, which combined a mostly eremetical with cenobitical life. Robert of Molesme established a very strict observance of the Benedictine life at Citeaux. Those who followed this reform were called Cistercians. William of Champeau formed the Victorines in Paris to promote a very disciplined form of religious life with a serious commitment to scholastic theology.

Ecclesiastical rivalry between the Christian East and West strained relationships between Constantinople and Rome. The temporary Photian schism in the ninth century led eventually to the sad long-term rupture and the separation of the Orthodox churches from Rome in 1054.

St. Bernard of Clairvaux

As the eleventh century was coming to a close, Bernard was born in 1090 to a noble family in Dijon in south-eastern France. He was the third of seven children and experienced a very close relationship with his mother. She insisted on a clerical school education for him even though his brothers all became either farmers or soldiers. Bernard's mother died when he was about seventeen years of age. At twenty-two years of age, Bernard presented himself to the monastery that Robert of Molesne had established in Citeaux. This monastery had been struggling to survive. But Bernard, who revealed early on his charm and charisma, persuaded thirty relatives and friends to accompany him to Citeaux. He gave himself unstintingly to the life, even injuring his health with his austere embrace of the discipline.

Bernard became the novice master at Citeaux. Then, as the monastery continued to grow, the abbot appointed him as the first abbot of a new foundation at Clairvaux. While serving as abbot, Bernard made seventy new foundations from Clairvaux, and ninety-four further foundations came from those seventy!

Despite Bernard's commitment to the strict monastic life, he also became actively involved in the wider life of the Church. He engaged publicly in a debate with Peter the Venerable of Cluny over the interpretation of the Rule of St. Benedict. Bernard was convinced that Cluny had made too many accommodations to the life of the world. He also participated in a public quarrel with Abelard over Abelard's approach to the interpretation of Sacred Scripture and his promotion of the scholastic study of theology. Bernard was convinced that Abelard's more scientific study of Sacred Scripture and his scholastic approach to theology were robbing both of the spiritual soul that should animate them. Because Bernard adopted the approach of the earlier Fathers of the Church in his own preaching and writing, he is often called the last of the Fathers.

Five Books on Consideration

Bernard was a prolific preacher and writer. On the priesthood alone, he published four treatises. The one that has become a classic is entitled *Five Books on Consideration*.[1] This is really one treatise with five sections written at varying intervals as time would allow. He wrote this at the behest of Pope Eugene III. Bernard had been a mentor of Eugene as he assumed the role of abbot of the Cistercian Monastery of San Andrea at Tre Fontane on the outskirts of Rome. Eugene, who was a simple man and overwhelmed with his election, wanted Bernard to help him move into this new role with all the administrative responsibilities connected to it in a way that would be pleasing to God. Of all of Bernard's writing on the priesthood or the episcopacy, this merits special attention because it addressed the challenge of fidelity to a spiritual life amid complex and demanding administrative concerns.

Bernard asked Pope Eugene to send him a copy of his calendar before he wrote the first section. Eugene had then been in office four years. Bernard, after reviewing the calendar, detailing the way the pope was living his life, focused on urging Pope Eugene to keep in mind that his calling was first and foremost to be a spiritual father, not a

---

[1] Bernard of Clairvaux, *Five Books on Consideration*, Cistercian Fathers Series, trans. John Anderson and Elizabeth Kennan, vol. 2 (Kalamazoo, MI: Cistercian Publications, 1976).

feudal lord.[2] By this time Eugene was trying to get a hold of his temporal duties as governor of the Papal States. Bernard feared Eugene would become so engaged in external issues that his role in spiritual leadership would suffer. Eugene's efforts faced extremely difficult and frustrating challenges because of the feuding among the people. In fact a disproportionate percentage of his time was consumed in exercising the role of chief justice to settle the disputes and rivalries among various factions.[3] Moreover, he served as ultimate court of appeal for all cases unsatisfactorily decided by lower courts. Bernard urged both discernment and delegation on the part of the pope: discernment to select those cases that truly impacted the mission of the Church, then delegation to other trustworthy subordinates all other cases.[4] Thus, Bernard pressed Pope Eugene to revise his pattern of life so that he would have much more time for prayerful *consideration* about the more important responsibilities that were his.[5] In effect, Bernard urged the pope to develop a rule of life, not shaped by his previous monastic life, but still inspired by that life.[6] The purpose would be the same, but the responsibilities and, therefore, the order of the day significantly different.

Then a year later, Bernard wrote Book II. After the Muslim defeat of the Christians at Edessa, Pope Eugene had called for a Christian crusade to win back control of the sacred shrines in the Holy Land so that Christian pilgrims could visit them safely. The pope had asked Bernard to preach that crusade in order to encourage participation in it and support of it. The crusade proved to be a huge disaster.

[2] Ibid., I, 22–23.
[3] Ibid., I, 3–4.
[4] Ibid., I, 6–7.
[5] Ibid., I, 7–8.
[6] Ibid., 9.

This perplexed and humbled Bernard, who had been confident God would enable the crusaders to be victorious. So
the first part of Book II contains Bernard's own reflection on
how to interpret this defeat. He wondered if the crusaders
had engaged in immoral behavior, displeasing to God. In any
case, he reminded Pope Eugene that he should remember
that the Israelites, too, had to suffer many setbacks before
they were able to reach the Promised Land.[7]

Then Bernard launched into a strong exhortation,
encouraging Pope Eugene never to lose sight of his need
to *consider* carefully in an ongoing way the truth about
himself. Bernard had already written the treatise *The Steps
of Humility*,[8] a series of monastic conferences on the sev-
enth chapter in the Rule of St. Benedict. He now urged
Eugene to live the truth about himself: what he was (an
ordinary man); who he was (an elected pope); what kind
of person he was becoming (his life of virtue or vice).[9]
Thus, Bernard wanted Pope Eugene never to forget his
origins as he reflected regularly on the kind of man he
was becoming in the exercise of his sacred ministry in the
Church.[10] This consideration was for the sake of humility.

Two years later, Bernard wrote Book III. This section
focused on the truth about those entrusted to his care.
Bernard urged Pope Eugene to *consider* carefully both the
clergy and laity of Rome as well as the faithful in the universal Church.[11] He emphasized his special need first to be
a good spiritual father to the members of the Diocese of
Rome. This had to involve confronting ambition, greed,
sexual misconduct, and the misuse of his office by constant

[7] Ibid., II, 1.

[8] See Bernard of Clairvaux, *The Steps of Humility*, trans. George Bosworth
Burch (Cambridge, MA: Harvard University Press, 1942).

[9] *Five Books on Consideration* II, 2–14.

[10] Ibid., II, 9.

[11] Ibid., III, 2–5.

appeals to him about purely secular matters.[12] This consideration was in service to loving pastoral care.

In Book IV, written shortly thereafter, Bernard pleaded with Pope Eugene to *consider* carefully his principal collaborators. Were the members of the papal curia and the papal household wise and mature? Did they understand the primary responsibility of the pope as a spiritual father, or were they continually drawing him unnecessarily into temporal affairs? Bernard urged Eugene to discern whether those in place had originally been good choices and whether new candidates being considered for office were truly men of God and of the Church. This discernment required the elimination of those who were sycophants or manipulators.[13] This consideration was in service to the choice of wise and virtuous collaborators.

Finally, Bernard wrote Book V. This time the *consideration* turned heavenward. In the early books, Bernard had recognized that the busy life of a pope would usually mean that prayer would be more *consideration* than *contemplation*. For Bernard, *consideration* meant a form of reflective meditation on the realities impinging on his ministry. In this final book, Bernard hoped that he might also find prayerful moments of *contemplation*.

Some Implications

St. Bernard, in his guidance to Pope Eugene III, grappled with the very real challenges that a bishop or pastor has to face as he tries to fulfill his administrative duties while ensuring fidelity to his spiritual responsibilities as well. Unfortunately, the demands of administration often

[12] Ibid., III, 2–4.
[13] Ibid., IV, 2, 4.

so overwhelmed bishops and priests that the spiritual focus became lost. Sadly, this led too many to become worldly feudal lords rather than good spiritual fathers. Pope Eugene did not want to fall into that trap. That is why he asked Bernard for spiritual guidance.

Bernard's response encouraged Pope Eugene to address the triple truth about himself, others, and God. He urged Eugene to keep before his eyes his humanity, his baptismal identity, and his papal role as he reflected on the truth about himself. He urged wise discretion in his choice of collaborators and wide-eyed understanding of the true needs of the faithful in his meditation on others. When it came to God, Bernard urged Eugene not to seek the truth *about* God, but rather the truth *of* God. The truth *about* God is theology; the truth *of* God is contemplation.[14] Bernard earnestly hoped that Eugene could bring from his previous monastic life a desire to call upon the angels in the hope of being able at times to contemplate the length (eternity), the breadth (charity), the height (majesty), and the depth (wisdom) of God[15]—thus did St. Bernard hope to help his disciple Pope Eugene to enter faithfully and fully into that expression of spiritual fatherhood which would allow administrative responsibilities to fall better into their proper place. This is a wonderful vade mecum for busy pastors!

Lord Jesus, who revealed the face of the Father in your life and public ministry to others, help me, through the intercession of St. Bernard of Clairvaux, to approach the administrative responsibilities you give to me as a spiritual father, less concerned about managerial tasks and more eager to express your saving love for your people. Grant this is your own name. Amen.

[14] Ibid., V, 3.
[15] Ibid., V, 13.

Chapter 7

St. Thomas Aquinas: Awe before the Eucharistic Mystery

The Thirteenth Century

Some remarkable developments characterized the thirteenth century. Monastic and cathedral schools had rendered a very important service in handing on the accumulated wisdom rooted in Sacred Scripture and reflected on in the writings of the Fathers of the Church. But a more scientific approach to learning had given rise to a number of universities. They started exploring issues in urban life and preparing students for professional careers. Thus, universities became renowned for specific areas of study: philosophy and theology in Paris; law in Bologna; science and mathematics in Oxford; science and philosophy in Cologne; medicine in Salerno.

The faith of the people found expression in the construction of magnificent Gothic cathedrals. These churches seemed to reach to the skies in testimony to God's transcendent glory. Talented architects and artisans worked together to create masterpieces that encouraged worship and also provided a visual catechesis for a mostly illiterate people. These edifices required great sacrifice and extended labor over generations.

As the feudal society continued to mingle secular with sacred responsibilities in the lives of Church leaders, Catholic culture flourished, but Gospel living suffered. The faithful developed a remarkable reverence and awe toward the presence of the Lord in the Eucharist. Although poorly catechized in their faith and especially in the fuller meaning of the Mass, they became focused on the wonder of the Eucharistic Presence. This led not only to the need for many priests to celebrate Masses but also to the desire for more opportunities to adore Christ in the Blessed Sacrament outside of Mass. More priests were ordained as "Mass priests", but with little scriptural and theological preparation for preaching.

In this atmosphere, Francis of Assisi and Dominic de Guzman introduced a new form of religious life in the Church. They combined some elements of monastic life with a more mobile availability for pastoral ministry, while placing special emphasis on witnessing to a life closer to the Gospel. Dominic sought to compensate for the limited education and preparation of parish priests for preaching by developing a community of well-formed preachers of the faith. Francis, on the other hand, focused especially on Gospel simplicity. He wanted his friars to preach the Gospel more by their way of life. Both religious founders sought to bring renewed life to the Church through a return to the evangelical virtues of poverty, chastity, and obedience. Because of their dependence on the free-will offerings of the faithful rather than on ecclesiastical benefices, both orders were called mendicant.

These renewal initiatives became counterpoints to some of the misguided movements that arose in the wake of the widespread worldliness and moral laxity in the lives of many Church leaders. The Cathars or Albigensians (so-called because of their association with the French town of Albi) promoted exaggerated expressions of fasting. The Waldensians (who took their name from Peter Waldo of Lyon) promoted an exaggerated expression of poverty. The Dominicans and Franciscans provided authentic and orthodox alternatives to these well-meaning, but heretical, reform movements.

Political developments also paved the way for the breakdown of a united European Christendom. The French king Philip Augustus won a victory over the Holy Roman Emperor Otto IV at the Battle of Bouvines in 1214. This was the first of a number of other national movements. The greater threat to European Christendom continued to come from the Muslim Moors in Spain. They sought further expansion into Europe. Meanwhile the European world was becoming more aware of an Asiatic world that had not yet been explored or evangelized.

St. Thomas Aquinas

This was the world into which Thomas of Aquino was born in 1225. He first experienced schooling with the Benedictines at Monte Cassino. But at fourteen years of age he moved to Naples. This meant movement from a monastic setting to a city setting, from feudal society to large city society. It was here that he first studied Aristotle.

It was also in Naples that he met the Dominicans and the evangelical movement. Despite strong family opposition, Thomas joined the Dominicans. They sent him to study at the University of Paris. It was there that he met and studied under the Dominican Albert the Great, scientist and philosopher.

When Albert moved to the University of Cologne, he invited Thomas to join him to help set up a theological faculty there as well. A few years later, Thomas was offered a chair in theology at the University of Paris and returned for a while. But he tired of the faculty political squabbles and accepted appointments as a papal curial teacher in Orvieto, Rome, and Viterbo. Then he returned for a short time to the University of Paris. But, once again, he was happy to leave the conflicted faculty there to accept the role as Chair of the theology faculty at the University of Naples. It was at Naples that Pope Gregory X asked Thomas to prepare theological study that would aid in the proposed reunion of the Eastern Christian churches with Rome at the upcoming Council of Lyon. Thomas died en route to the Council in the Monastery of Fossa Nuova in 1274. The Council reached an agreement between Pope Gregory X and Patriarch Michael VIII. But this union was later repudiated by Patriarch Michael's successor Andronicus II.

Thomas was a prolific writer of theology, including commentaries on the *Sentences* of Peter Lombard, on Sacred Scripture, and on the works of Aristotle. He wrote philosophical and theological treatises on a number of topics. He addressed the issues raised by the schism between the Eastern and Western Christian churches. He wrote a masterful work for those who do not believe the Christian faith. But his masterpiece was the *Summa Theologiae*,[1]

---

[1] Thomas Aquinas, *Summa Theologiae*, trans. Fathers of the English Province (New York: Benzinger Brothers, 1922).

which synthesized the doctrine of the faith for Christians. Shortly before completing this *Summa*, Thomas experienced on December 6, 1273, a vision in prayer that led him to be convinced that all his writing was but "straw" in light of the reality of who God is. Because of this, he never finished the *Summa*. His secretary and collaborator, Reginald of Piperno, after Thomas' death, drew from his *Commentary on the Sentences of Peter Lombard* to complete the *Summa Theologiae*. Unfortunately, the two sacraments that Thomas never included in the *Summa* were Holy Orders and Matrimony.[2] Hence, the Church has the work of the young Thomas, not the mature Thomas, on the subject of the priesthood.

St. Thomas and the Priesthood

In the *Summa Theologiae Supplement*, Thomas was concerned about commenting on Peter Lombard's treatment of the then prevalent speculative issues regarding Holy Orders. Thus, Thomas recognized Christ to be *the* priest of the New Covenant. He treated the ordained in relationship to the Eucharist.[3] He considered the ministry of the Word in relation to the Eucharist.[4] He struggled with the sacramentality of the episcopacy because it did not involve any new relationship to or power over the Eucharist.[5] In this treatment, the Church does not have the benefit of Thomas' more mature reflection. But he systematized the prevalent views of his day.

St. Thomas made a significant contribution to priestly pastoral care in the way in which he treated moral theology

[2] Ibid., III Suppl., qq. 34–68.
[3] Ibid., III, q. 37.
[4] Ibid., III, q. 36, 2.
[5] Ibid., III, q. 40.

in the *Summa Theologiae*.[6] He imitated St. Paul in recognizing that Christian morality flows from faith reality. Thus, he tried to help priests become good confessors, even as he directed all his theological writing to encourage a pastoral apologetics, catechesis, and homiletics.

Moreover, Thomas made a significant contribution to the spirituality of ordained priesthood in his poetic and liturgical compositions on the one hand and his way of living priesthood on the other.

For Thomas, the mystery of the Eucharist is the center of all Christian faith life. The Trinitarian mystery in itself and the Triune God's work of creation and redemption are fully expressed in the Eucharist. So, the ordained priest, to whom this gift is entrusted in a unique way, must live his whole life oriented toward this mystery. Pope Urban IV asked Thomas and Bonaventure in 1264 to submit a proposed liturgical text for the new Feast of Corpus Christi, which he was instituting. When Bonaventure read Thomas' text, he tore up his proposed text. It is from Thomas that we have not only the liturgical prayers for the Solemnity of the Body and Blood of the Lord but also the *Verbum Supernum*, *Pange Lingua*, *Tantum Ergo*, *O Salutaris Hostia*, *Lauda Sion Salvatorem*, and *Adoro Te Devote*. These hymns express in succinct theological but also beautifully poetic language the sacramental mystery of faith.

Thomas Aquinas wanted priests to study well and pray well in order to preach well. He embraced fully the Dominican motto, *contemplata aliis tradere* (to hand on to others the fruits of one's contemplation). For Thomas, prayer was a precondition for good theological study. He prayed over Sacred Scripture. He pondered the witness of the Fathers.

[6] Ibid., II.

He meditated on the magisterial teaching of the Church. He studied the best in scientific and philosophical thought about the world. He did all of this in union with Mary. He called her the *triclinium totius Trinitatis* (the abiding place of the Blessed Trinity).

Thomas witnessed in his own life to the renewal that the mendicant orders wanted so much to bring to the Church. He embraced simplicity of life. He remained faithful to chaste life and love in continuity with his early victory over sexual temptation, presented to him by his brother and a prostitute. He never accepted any appointment apart from the explicit approval of his religious superiors and willingly complied with the requests that popes made of him in life.

Some Implications

St. Thomas Aquinas, although not a diocesan priest, had a remarkable sense of ecclesial ministry. He wanted priests to take the study of theology very seriously, while still subordinating this study to experiential communion with God through contemplation. He was eager to pursue the truth wherever it could be found in the search for Divine Truth. He modeled for all time what it means to enter sympathetically into dialogue with those with whom one might not agree, by first exhibiting the humility of appreciating what has led the other to a different conclusion. As a result of this patient listening and learning, he could then more fruitfully teach the truth with charity.

Thomas' mind and heart were open to truth wherever it could be found. He had a deep appreciation for science, philosophy, and theology. He learned science from Albert the Great. He drew on the ancient pagan philosophers,

Muslim philosophers, and Eastern Church theologians to grow in understanding and expressing the truth. Thomas was not so much a creative thinker as a prayerful original thinker who could synthesize and systematize the available knowledge of his day in service to a deeper engagement of the truth. For Thomas, truth was not abstract. It was and is life-giving. For living the truth means living in communion with Truth himself, the Word of God. To be a disciple of the Truth is to be a disciple of the Lord.

Moreover, Thomas witnessed in his own life to the way that simplicity of life, chaste love, and humble obedience offer powerful credibility to priestly teaching and preaching.

Lord Jesus, who revealed the mystery of your life in the Sacrament of the Holy Eucharist, grant through the intercession of St. Thomas Aquinas that I may always grow in greater communion with you in your Body and your Blood and feed your people with your life and your truth both in word and in action. Grant this in your own name. Amen.

Chapter 8

Martin Luther: The Power of the Word of God

The Sixteenth Century

Many factors coalesced in the sixteenth century to cause a perfect storm. After the significant achievements of the thirteenth century, the following two centuries had experienced a decline in the understanding and vigor of Catholic faith. The mendicant orders continued to thrive. The earlier monastic orders—Benedictines, Augustinians, and Carmelites—still attracted members. But the quality of faith life among the people suffered. Parish priests were often ill-prepared to preach. Simony, sexual immorality, and greed often marred the way in which diocesan priests lived their lives. Popes and members of the papal curia sometimes lived very secular and immoral lives.

During the repeated waves of the Black Plague, nearly one-third of the European population died. Mystery plays rather than sound doctrine provided the people with the spiritual support they sought. The Great Western Schism (1378–1417), wherein there were competing claimants to the office of Peter in Rome and Avignon, undermined the respect for the papacy. Scholastic theology that had flourished so well in the thirteenth century began to suffer from intellectual conflicts between Platonists and Aristotleians, Augustinians, and Thomists. William of Ockham called into question the possibility of reaching universal truth. Socially, the feudal structures of society were crumbling as cities and national states became more powerful.

In the midst of this turbulence, God did raise up some remarkable figures who tried valiantly to offer spiritual leadership and guidance to a confused people: Meister Eckhart, Jans Ruysbroeck, John Tauler, and Henry Suso in the Lowlands; Walter Hilton, Richard Rolle, Julian of Norwich in England; Catherine of Siena in Italy; Thomas à Kempis and the *Devotio Moderna* in the Lowlands, France, and Germany. Saintly men and women strove to offer spiritual guidance when the institutional expressions of the Church were failing.

Among these remarkable leaders who contributed to the needed renewal and made a special contribution to the reform of the clergy was St. John of Avila. Pope Benedict, in naming him a Doctor of the Church in 2012, said: "If Master Avila was a pioneer in pointing to the universal call to holiness, he also had an essential role in the historical development of a systematic doctrine on the priesthood. Down the centuries his writings have been a source of inspiration for priestly spirituality and even a current of mysticism among secular priests. His influence can clearly be seen in a number of later spiritual writers."[1]

[1] Benedict XVI, Apostolic Letter Proclaiming Saint John of Avila, Diocesan Priest, a Doctor of the Universal Church (October 7, 2012), taken from *L'Osservatore Romano*, weekly edition in English, October 31, 2012, https://www.ewtn.com/catholicism/library/john-of-avila-preacher-and-spiritual-master-6671.

But, as the sixteenth century ushered in the cultural Renaissance and an explosion of new forms of scientific enquiry, a humanism not always connected to faith began to emerge. A wave of optimism about the potential of human beings and the possibility of human progress washed over Europe. Release from the many social and economic strictures of feudal structures awakened a sense of freedom previously not imagined. The invention of the printing press in 1453 made possible a revolutionary new approach to the communication of ideas and ideologies.

Martin Luther

This was the world into which Martin Luther was born in 1483 in Thuringia, Germany. His was a religiously prac-ticing Catholic family. His father was poor and strict. He provided his son with an early exposure to the popular piety of one of the schools conducted by adherents to the *Devotio Moderna*. This expression of Christian spirituality was affective and Christocentric, but suspicious of aca-demic theology. Luther went on to study at the University of Erfurt, where he came into contact with the humanism of the Renaissance and the philosophical teaching of Wil-liam of Ockham. At Erfurt he began to study law.

It is not clear how Luther changed course and decided to enter a very strict house of the Augustinians in Erfurt in 1505. He certainly absorbed the faith from his parents and family. He also experienced a serious personal sickness, a frighteningly close call with a lightning strike in a thunder-storm, and the death of a close friend. Any of these may have impacted his decision as well.

Because of his earlier intellectual studies, Martin Luther was advanced to priestly ordination in only two years. He was assigned to teach moral theology in Wittenberg and then given the opportunity to earn a doctorate in theology in order to teach Sacred Scripture there as well. In this role, he taught the Psalms as well as St. Paul's letters to the Romans, Galatians, and Hebrews from 1513 to 1518.

During those same years of teaching, Martin Luther experienced a serious spiritual struggle. He seems to have been tortured by moral scruples. The Sacrament of Penance and Reconciliation became very painful for him. While involved in this struggle, he made a trip to Rome with his former professor and mentor, Father Staupitz, and became scandalized by the lives of the Roman clergy and some of the Curia. Upon his return, Luther began to develop a theory about justification, impacted by his study and teaching of Romans and Galatians. This theory focused on the role of God's grace and faith in God. It brought him more relief from his scruples than the Sacrament of Confession.

When Pope Leo X was building St. Peter's Basilica in Rome, he attached an indulgence under certain conditions to gifts made in support of this effort. A Dominican friar, Father Johann Tetzel, became the papal preacher of this cause in Germany. Martin Luther objected to this preaching, which he considered was promoting the purchase of indulgences through monetary gifts to this cause. On October 31, 1517, Luther released ninety-five theses, which some claim he posted on the door of the Wittenberg cathedral. His release of these theses was the usual way for a university professor to invite theological debate. The Archbishop of Mainz, who was working with Pope Leo X in the promotion of these indulgences, denounced Luther to Rome. Luther met with Father Cajetan, Superior General of the Dominican Order, to discuss the issues involved. Luther refused to recant. Father Cajetan recommended that he be called to Rome for an ecclesiastical trial. But on June 15, 1520, Pope Leo X issued a bull of excommunication, *Exsurge Domine*. Although the excommunication took place on that date, the Protestant Reformation is usually associated with the publication of the theses in 1517.

Pope Leo X's abrupt excommunication made reconciliation much more difficult. During the subsequent five years, Martin Luther developed his convictions about Scripture alone (dismissing any normative role for Sacred Tradition or magisterial teaching), grace alone (focusing on God's initiative apart from human cooperation), and faith alone (the acceptance of God's grace without the need for virtuous works). He also began to express his growing convictions, which called into question the scriptural foundation for all the sacraments except Baptism and the Lord's Supper and challenged the need for ordination for those called to public ministry in the Church. In 1525, he married a former nun who bore him six children.

Luther and Church Ministry

In the letter *Concerning the Ministry*,[2] written in 1523 to the people of Prague, Luther revealed how far his thinking had developed regarding ordained priesthood. He was addressing a situation in Bohemia, where many of their bishops and priests had been interdicted because of their disobedience regarding the distribution of Holy Communion under both species. The interdict meant that any new candidate for the priesthood had to be sent to Rome to be ordained. This riled the Bohemian faithful. Luther offered them his teaching to provide them with an alternative.

[2] Martin Luther, *Concerning the Ministry*, in *Luther's Works*, ed. Helmet Lehmann and Conrad Bergendoff, vol. 40 (Philadelphia: Fortress Press, 1958).

In this letter, Luther claimed that each of the responsibilities of an ordained priest could also be performed by
a lay person. He justified his claim in the following ways.
Since lay people can teach their children, they should also
be able to preach.[3] Since lay people can baptize in an emergency, they should also be able to be an ordinary minister
of Baptism.[4] Since, as Luther claimed without scriptural
support, others besides the apostles were present at the Last
Supper, lay people should also be able to celebrate the sacrament of the Last Supper.[5] He also claimed that this was
confirmed by the fact that the New Testament does not
use the term *priest* in relation to the Eucharist.[6] Since the
keys for binding and loosing were also given to the whole
Church (Mt 16:18–19), all Christians should be able to
forgive sins.[7] Since only spiritual sacrifice is needed and
both Peter and Paul ascribe this to the lay priesthood (1 Pet
2:5; Rom 12:1), there is no need to ordain priests for this.[8]

History teaches us that any realistic possibility of reconciling with Martin Luther died with the bull of excommunication. When that happened, Luther appealed to a
council of the Church. Pope Leo X was not open to this.
Pope Adrian VI, not physically well, died within two years
of his election. Pope Clement VII had difficulty moving
forward because of an ongoing war between France and
the German emperor. Pope Paul III made the opening
of a council a main goal of his pontificate. But Luther,
by this time, had introduced unacceptable conditions for
his participation: the deliberations would have to draw on

[3] Ibid., 21–22.
[4] Ibid., 23.
[5] Ibid., 24.
[6] Ibid.
[7] Ibid., 25.
[8] Ibid., 28.

Sacred Scripture alone in the making of decisions; lay people needed to be included with an equal right to vote as bishops; the pope himself or a delegate could not be present at the sessions.

Some Implications

It is sad that efforts at reconciliation did not bear fruit. Serious mistakes on both sides frustrated the efforts. But Luther was right to restore an emphasis on the one unique priesthood of Christ, the sacramental share in that priesthood made possible to all the faithful in Baptism, the fundamental equality in Christian dignity of all the faithful, as well as the importance of all the faithful to engage in teaching the faith to their children, offering themselves in spiritual sacrifice, and witnessing to the Gospel in their lives. He also rightly focused on the incredible importance of good preaching on the part of those serving the priesthood of the laity.

But, unfortunately, Luther did not recognize that it was one thing to call those ordained in the Church to be what they are supposed to be, but quite another to claim that Christ did not give to his Church apostles who from the beginning exercised an authoritative role, expressed in a ministry to Word, sacrament, and pastoral governance. Moreover, the Fathers of the Church testify to the scriptural roots of each of the seven sacraments. The ministry of Word is profoundly related to the ministry of sacrament and comes to special fulfillment in sacrament. In order to appreciate the fullness of teaching on Holy Orders, it is necessary to appreciate how the early Church bishops and Fathers interpreted Sacred Scripture and applied the Word of God to ecclesial life.

Fortunately, constructive theological dialogue between Catholics and Lutherans has borne good fruit in developing a common statement on justification, a shared appreciation of the priesthood of the faithful, and the need for a public ministry of Word, sacrament, and pastoral care in the Church. Luther has helped restore an appropriate emphasis on the ministry of the Word. But significant differences regarding the ordained priesthood still prevail about the qualifications and selection of candidates for public ministry; the sacramental nature of this ministry; the threefold degrees of Holy Orders; the nature of apostolicity; and the role of the papacy. The differences become particularly evident in the way in which each approaches the mystery of the Eucharist. In recent years, many Lutherans have also compromised the Gospel teaching on human sexual morality and now gender theory.

While remaining faithful to the whole of God's revelation, it is still important for the Church to welcome Luther's focus on the irreplaceable significance of the inspired Word of God in the Bible. The ordained need to be immersed in the Bible in their prayer, and then preach the Word of God with wisdom, conviction, even boldness. The renewal of the ordained priesthood in any age requires a profound engagement with the Word of God and an ever greater commitment to proclaiming it with understanding and zeal.

Lord Jesus, who as the Word-made-flesh revealed the fullness of divine revelation during your historical life on earth, help me to receive you, the Word of Life, in my mind and heart so that I may fulfill the ministry of the Word entrusted to me in a faithful, saving way and lead your people to the sacramental expression of your Word. Grant this in your own name. Amen.

Chapter 9

The Council of Trent: Seminary Formation
for a Ministry of Word, Sacrament,
and Pastoral Care

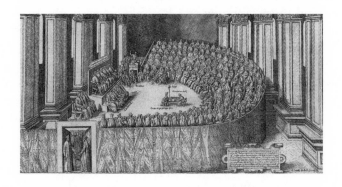

The Struggle for Catholic Reformation

The last chapter provided an understanding of how the
imploding political and social structures, the deteriorating
ecclesial life, the new scientific adventures and discoveries,
the intellectual awakening that accompanied the Renaissance quest for human development and freedom, and
the shift in academic study from a focus on God to man
coalesced to provide the context for the Protestant Reformation. Some would suggest that even if Martin Luther
did not emerge, someone else would have led a Protestant
Reformation. Two such persons did emerge quickly: John

Calvin (1509–1564), a theologian, pastor, and reformer, and Huldrych Zwingli (1484–1531), another leader of the Reformation, both based in Switzerland.

There were also some important reform initiatives focused on priestly life and ministry among those who remained faithful in the Catholic Church. Reginald Cardinal Pole of England started a seminary on his own even before the Council of Trent. The saintly Bishop Bartholomew of the Martyrs, in Braga, Portugal, engaged in serious efforts to prepare his priests to preach the Word of God more faithfully and fruitfully, even in the face of opposition. He laid the groundwork for a seminary before Trent. Charles Borromeo, later the saintly Bishop of Milan, Italy, developed a series of proposals for the reform of the clergy. Some clergy reform efforts led to the formation of new religious communities: the Oratory of Divine Love in Rome, the Theatines in Chieti, the Somaschi in Venice, and the Barnabites in Milan.

There was no great papal enthusiasm for a council. But Martin Luther had made an appeal of the papal excommunication to a council. As narrated in the last chapter, after the futile efforts of his predecessors, Pope Paul III made it a priority of his pontificate, still with the hope that Martin Luther and his followers would participate. The German emperor had assured the pope that he would make every effort to persuade Luther to agree. But the requirements upon which Luther insisted—the exclusion of the pope or his delegate; the restriction of theological sources for deliberations and decisions to the Bible; and equal voting rights for lay participants with the bishops—became unsurmountable hurdles. In response to Luther's request that the council take place in German territory, not in the Papal States, Paul III settled on Trent as neutral territory between the two.

The Council of Trent

The Council of Trent formally opened in 1545, twenty-five years after the excommunication of Luther with the stated goals to heal the confessional differences, to reform the Church, and to establish peace and a united approach to handling the threats of the Ottoman Turks. But by the time the bishops gathered in Trent, it became obvious that Martin Luther, whose conditions for participation could not be accepted, would not come. Hence, the possibility of reconciliation suffered an early death.

John O'Malley in his book *Trent: What Happened at the Council*[1] provides a detailed account of the challenging road the Council travelled. Reluctant episcopal participation, squabbles over the agenda, a typhus epidemic, political pressures, the deaths of Pope Paul III and Pope Julius III, and ecclesiastical feuds all played a role in a three-part, eighteen-year experience. It was only in the last two years as Cardinal Pole assumed the role of Papal Legate for the newly elected Pope Paul IV that amazing order emerged from dizzying chaos. The Holy Spirit ultimately enabled the bishops to come together in adopting very significant doctrinal teaching, in rejecting those elements in Reformation preaching that were contrary to this teaching, and in instituting the sweeping decrees that called for new ecclesiastic discipline and norms for genuine reform in the Church.

Trent's treatment of the reform of the ordained priesthood was scattered through a number of the sessions of the Council. But the principal doctrinal teaching on the ordained priesthood appeared in Session XXIII. Holy

---

[1] John O'Malley, *Trent: What Happened at the Council* (Cambridge, MA: Harvard University Press, 2013).

Orders, the Council taught, was indeed instituted by Christ as evidenced in the New Testament (explicitly) for priesthood and the diaconate.[2] It is indeed a sacrament.[3] The ordained priesthood impresses a sacramental character or seal on the recipient, distinguishing him from the baptismal priesthood.[4] Bishops have a special role in spiritual governance that is independent of any civil power.[5]

This teaching followed right after the doctrinal teaching on the Eucharist in Session XXII. The Council affirmed that the Holy Sacrifice of the Mass was instituted by Christ as testified to in the New Testament.[6] The Mass is propitiatory for the living and the dead[7] and is offered to God, not to the saints whose intercession is invoked.[8] Participation in the Mass is principally through interior engagement in prayer.[9] The bread and wine are truly transubstantiated into the Body and Blood of the Lord.[10]

The Council promoted the reform of priestly life and ministry through many disciplinary decrees. Some of them ensured true pastoral care of souls by requiring bishops and priests to live in the actual territory of the people they served[11] and to limit themselves to one ministry from which they would derive sustenance.[12] Bishops were to ensure that priests were living faithful moral lives.[13] The

[2] *The Canons and Decrees of the Council of Trent*, trans. and ed. H.J. Schroeder Jr. (St. Louis, MO: B. Herder Book Company, 1955), Session XXIII, Chap. 1.
[3] Ibid., Chap. 3.
[4] Ibid., Chap. 4.
[5] Ibid.
[6] Ibid., Session XXII, Chap. 1.
[7] Ibid., Chap. 2.
[8] Ibid., Chap. 3.
[9] Ibid., Chap. 5.
[10] Ibid., Chap. 2.
[11] Ibid., Sessions VI and XXIII.
[12] Ibid., Session VII.
[13] Ibid., Sessions XIII and XXII.

Council called for financial regulations that would penal-
ize mismanagement or financial corruption.[14] Bishops and
priests were to make every effort to get to know and care
for the faithful under their care[15] and to nurture a special
care for the poor.[16] In order to ensure that candidates for
the priesthood would be properly formed, the Council
called for the establishment of seminaries.[17] This last initiative provided for the development of the most effective
way to reform priestly formation.

The more important disciplinary decrees focused on
restoring the prayerful study of Sacred Scripture to a special place in ordained ministry so that bishops and priests
might preach knowledgeably, insightfully, and persuasively. To this end the Council called for the establishment
of lectureships in Sacred Scripture at each cathedral,[18] the
preparation of priestly candidates with sufficient knowledge,[19] and the appointment of assistants to existing pastors
ill-prepared to preach so that these vicars could preach for
them.[20] The ordained were to explain to the faithful the
Mass, each of the sacraments, and all the faith and moral
teaching necessary for living the Christian life.[21]

Thus, the Council tackled the crisis in the ordained
priesthood in the sixteenth century by restating the received
revelation on those teachings the reformers were denying
and by providing for the supervised discipline of the lives
of those preparing for the priesthood or already ordained.
This set the agenda for a true Catholic Reformation.

[14] Ibid., Session XXII.
[15] Ibid., Session XXIII.
[16] Ibid.
[17] Ibid., Session XVIII.
[18] Ibid., Session V.
[19] Ibid., Session VII.
[20] Ibid., Session XXI.
[21] Ibid., Session XXIV.

Those bishops who were already committed to reform before the Council led the way in implementing the disciplinary decrees of the Council. This was especially true of Cardinal Pole in Canterbury and Cardinal Borromeo in Milan. Pope Paul IV also enlisted Ignatius of Loyola and his newly founded Society of Jesus to embrace this mission for the Church as a whole. This request meant that the Jesuits would play a leading role in the acceptance and promotion of the Tridentine reform. For priests, this renewal was to be focused on the Eucharist. The implemented disciplinary decrees became instruments in service to more competent and worthy celebrants of the Eucharist.

Some Implications

The Council of Trent provides concrete evidence that it is possible to address a serious crisis in the Church in a responsible way. Diversity in theological opinions and pastoral practice do not need to paralyze the Church. The Holy Spirit made it possible for a remarkable reexpression of the Church's teaching on disputed issues and quite concrete measures to promote pastoral discipline.

The Council assumed a decisive role in the renewal of the Church, even though it took many years to implement the reform it envisioned. Under extremely unpromising circumstances, the Council Fathers were able to restate truths being either obscured or denied by the reformers and to adopt a truly meaningful plan for reform. Sound reform is best accomplished when it is accompanied by a clear affirmation of the doctrinal truths of faith.

Unfortunately, without the participation of the reformers, the goal of reconciliation with the followers of Luther never materialized. The divisions that took place at that time have led over time to an ever escalating number of new churches or ecclesial communities. When there is no central seat of unity, strong in both promoting unity and articulating what constitutes the truth in doctrine and practice, then fragmentation is inevitable. Incredible as it may seem, there are an estimated forty-four thousand Christian ecclesial communities in the world today. The Christian world has a long way to go to realize the prayer of the Lord Jesus at the Last Supper. "I do not pray for these only, but also for those who believe in me through their word, that they may all be one; even as you, Father, are in me, and I in you, that they may also be in us, so that the world may believe that you have sent me" (Jn 17:20–21).

The Council of Trent set the stage for a true spiritual renewal in the Catholic Church, but it accepted as a *fait accompli* serious divisions in Christianity and left to another time the development of a vision for moving forward in the evangelization of people living in a "modern" world.

Lord Jesus, who entrusted to your Church both life-giving truth and a way of life, help me shun anything that feeds division in your Church and to ensure that your truth and life are witnessed faithfully in me and lived faithfully in your people. Grant this in your own name. Amen.

Chapter 10

The French School of Spirituality: Immersion in the Mystery of Faith

The Historical Context

The Council of Trent completed its work in 1563. But in the previous year violent conflicts had already broken out in Europe. In France, these conflicts were between the Calvinists (called Huguenots there) and Catholics, and between the nobles and the Crown. Sporadic wars of religion convulsed the country until 1598, when the Treaty of Nantes brought temporary peace with a division of towns between Protestants and Catholics. The Third Estate (the French bourgeoisie) refused to accept the decrees of the Council of Trent because they considered this Roman legislation to be a threat to a more independent Gallican

86

Church. The Crown and the Assembly of the Clergy, however, did embrace the Tridentine reform. This resulted in the Protestants becoming allied with the nobles and the Catholics with the royalty. In 1621, Cardinal Richelieu, who had become the Chief Minister of Affairs under King Louis XIII, arbitrarily repossessed the Protestant towns. This led to another Protestant uprising in 1625. These open conflicts, with both political and religious factors motivating them, deepened and hardened the divisions in Christendom.

In the midst of all this turbulence, some Catholic clergy became involved in significant efforts to renew priestly life and to prepare better priests. Father Adrien Bourdoise founded a seminary at Saint-Nicolas du Chardonnet. Pierre Cardinal de Bérulle (1575–1629) established a series of oratories for priests. Father Jean-Jacques Olier instituted a seminary, first in Vaugirard, then at St. Sulpice in Paris. Between 1612 and 1680 twenty seminaries opened their doors in France.

The French School of Spirituality

Cardinal de Bérulle is usually credited with being the founder of the French School of Spirituality. This spirituality was to animate priestly renewal and seminarian preparation not only in France but throughout a large segment of the Catholic Church in the following centuries. This French School of Spirituality first animated the seminaries in all of France. Following the Elizabethan persecution of Catholics in England and Ireland, most candidates for the priesthood in those countries were sent to French seminaries for their education and formation. All those who formed the faculty of early seminaries in the English

colonies, including America, were French Sulpicians, Vin-
centians, or Marists, imbued with the spirituality of this
French School.

Cardinal de Bérulle, although active in church-state
struggles at the time, was more of a contemplative at
heart. He was deeply spiritual. He had a profound impact
on Father Charles de Condren (1588–1641), whom he
appointed as the first Superior of his oratory. This oratory
brought together diocesan priests in Paris who wanted to
support one another in living a deeper spiritual life. Cardinal de Bérulle also influenced Father Jean-Jacques Olier
(1608–1659), founder of the Seminary of St. Sulpice.
Father Olier commented and expanded on the teaching
of both de Bérulle and de Condren in his own formation of
the seminarians. St. John Eudes (1601–1680) was a disciple of Cardinal de Bérulle. He promoted devotion to the
Sacred Heart of Jesus and the Immaculate Heart of Mary.
He founded a religious community that was both dedicated to this devotion and imbued with the spirituality of
the French School.

What was this spirituality?[1] It was rooted in Sacred
Scripture (especially the writings of St. Paul and St. John),
the Fathers of the Church (especially St. Augustine), and
the teaching of the Council of Trent. These writers tried to
provide the testimony of Sacred Scripture and the Fathers
as a way of bringing alive the systematic conciliar teaching.
They placed high priority on exploring and appreciating
the one all-encompassing Mystery of Faith. This Mystery
of Faith is preeminently Trinitarian: the one eternal act of
the Father's love for the Son and the Son's loving response
to the Father, expressed in the mutual gift of the Holy

[1] See John Barres, *Jean-Jacques Olier's Priestly Spirituality: Mental Prayer and
Virtues as the Foundation for the Direction of Souls* (Rome: Gregorian University
Press, 1999).

Spirit. This one internal and eternal Trinitarian act is expressed externally in the Father's loving missioning of the Son into the world to save it and the Son's loving response, made possible in the Holy Spirit. The external expression took historical form in the Incarnation, hidden life, public life, Passion, Death, Resurrection, and Ascension of the Lord and the descent of the Holy Spirit. For followers of the French School, the Lord Jesus constituted what they called "subsistent religion" (perfect worship of the Father in the Son). In his humanity, he is the perfect worshipper. He lived historically the *state* of Son of his Father while embracing interiorly the *disposition* or interior loving acceptance that this required. All Christians are invited in Baptism to participate in this Mystery of Faith through *adoration* of the Father, in *communion* with the Son, and by *cooperation* with the Holy Spirit.

Focus on the Priesthood

The ordained priest is called to serve this great Mystery of Faith for the sake of the people. Just as the Son of God through the hypostatic union with his humanity became *the* Priest, every ordained priest through the sacramental seal shares in the priesthood of Christ. Christ is the sacrament of God. The ordained priest is the sacrament of Christ. In exercising priestly ministry, the ordained priest, in a sense, "begets the Son" and joins in sending the Holy Spirit as he ministers sacramental life.

Thus, the ordained priest is a sacramental icon of Christ and his work is preeminently the work of redemption. This shapes all the ministry in which he is engaged. But it is especially expressed in the celebration of the Eucharist.

In order for ordained priests to live this out faithfully, they must be willing to enter into an ascetical effort that brings together this profound doctrine, the governing role entrusted to them in the Church, and holiness of life. Cardinal de Bérulle particularly lamented how in the preceding era the study of doctrine seemed to have become the role of theologians; the exercise of authority the role of bishops and pastors; holiness of life the pursuit of the religious.[2] Renewal required that these three become reunited in the life of the priest. In exercising authority, the priest reflects the Father; in prayerful study of the Word he enters into the Mystery of the Son; in acting in the Spirit he embraces holiness of life. Thus, the ordained priest grows in his *worship* of the Father, his *communion* with the Son, and his *cooperation* with the Holy Spirit in the Church's mission of salvation.

To do this, the ordained priest needs to share in the self-emptying of the Son of God (cf. Phil 2:5–11). This is very challenging because of fallen human nature. Priests, like all human beings, are inclined by original sin to self-exaltation, not self-abnegation. Priests must consciously foster a spirit of self-subservience before the Father, victimhood with the Son, and self-gift in humble service with the Holy Spirit.

Then, in order to support the theological virtues of faith, hope, and charity, the ordained priest needs to cultivate the moral virtue of humility and the practice of mortification. Humility keeps the priest from regarding himself as the center of attention or from living a privileged life. It attacks pride at its roots and makes growth in the other moral virtues more possible. The practice of mortification is needed to support the virtue of humility. Disordered desires, unfaced, lead the priest to greed for

[2] Pierre de Bérulle, *A Letter on the Priesthood, Bérulle and the French School*, ed. William Thompson, trans. Lowell Glendon Jr. (New York: Paulist Press, 1989).

power or money, lust for comfort or sexual gratification, and sloth in the spiritual struggle. Mortification aims to subdue those tendencies and increase the interior freedom to come alive to the redemptive love the Lord wants motivating his priests.

In this context, the ordained priest can better appreciate and live the evangelical virtues. First, he is called to a Gospel poverty. He is not to crave worldly possessions or honor. He is to live simply, making use of God's gifts in service to his mission. Second, he is called to live a chaste celibate love. This requires growth in inner self-control and human renunciation of sexual gratification. It has to be rooted in a love of the Lord above all. Third, the ordained priest is also called to obedience. Compliance with the Father's will, made manifest concretely in the direction of legitimate superiors, necessitates growing interior freedom. This freedom is not unrelated to the detachment from possessions and the detachment from pleasure involved in the other two virtues. Detachment from one's own will can be the most challenging to realize.

This spiritual journey needs ultimately to be directed to the zeal for souls. If the Lord's primary mission is redemption—if the Church's primary mission is to be the Lord's chosen vehicle for redemption—then the ordained priest must recognize that his primary mission is to be a humble servant of that redemptive mystery. This zeal for souls needs to flow from *agape*, the Lord's saving and sanctifying love for his people.

Some Implications

The French School of Spirituality offered an in-depth insight into the mystery of the Sacrament of Holy Orders. Its proponents recognized that the doctrinal teaching of

Trent and the disciplinary decrees of the same Council needed to be undergirded with a spirituality that would integrate and deepen their significance.

This spirituality, which recognized that the entire Mystery of Faith is not only represented in the Eucharist but is at the heart of all Christian faith, had a profound impact on the Catholic revival following both the period of the Enlightenment and the devastating experience of the Reign of Terror in France. It promoted an exalted understanding of the ordained priesthood. Even though it was intended to serve the salvation and sanctification of the lay faithful, it did not yet sufficiently address the relationship to the lay priesthood of the baptized. This had to wait until the Second Vatican Council. The teaching of this French spiritual renewal shaped the spiritual formation offered in many seminaries in the ensuing years. In fact it continued to impact the formation of priests up to the Second Vatican Council. This is the teaching that shaped the life and ministry of St. Jean Vianney, patron saint of all priests. It undergirds Sulpician spirituality. It was reflected in the writing of Abbot Columba Marmion and Archbishop Fulton Sheen.

Lord Jesus, who offer to me your saving and sanctifying grace in the Mystery of Faith, grant to me the virtues of humility and self-abnegation so I may become a faith-filled and faithful minister of your saving Mystery to others. Grant this in your own name. Amen.

Chapter 11

The Second Vatican Council: Ministerial Priesthood Serving Baptismal Priesthood

The Historical Context

The French School of Spirituality continued to impact the formation of priests up through the middle of the twentieth century. But considerable political upheaval in the eighteenth and nineteenth centuries presented challenges to the Church. The eighteenth century had given rise to the Enlightenment. Proponents of the Enlightenment hoped to bring an end to the religious wars in Europe by substituting human reason for faith. Many hoped that the triumph of reason over faith would rid the continent of these seemingly endless religious conflicts.

The American Revolution (1775–1783) ushered in a new era for democracy and an experiment in religious freedom. British dominance began to diminish. America's success in securing independence provided an impetus for peoples elsewhere to consider alternatives to living under a government controlled by royalty or despots.

The French Revolution (1789–1799) had a greater impact on Europe. The French pursuit of *fraternité*, *égalité*, and *liberté* caught the attention of many people hankering for a new order in society. But the meaning of these slogans was not always clear. Did *fraternité* mean living under a government elected by the people, or did it mean a rejection of all authority? Did *égalité* mean equality in human dignity or the forced elimination of all differences? Did *liberté* mean freedom from unjust rule or freedom from any objective norms? Bitter struggles, even political chaos, ensued because of this ambiguity. As the Church attempted to restore an appreciation for order, she became associated with the Ancien Régime. The revolutionaries resisted the Church's role and began to attack bishops, priests, and religious. Their goal, *laïcité*, encouraged strong anti-clerical feelings. Sometimes these led to open persecution. Religious communities were sometimes disbanded. Church property was seized. The faith of many was undermined as the government took over education.

Italy, too, experienced its struggles. Some nationalists began a struggle to unify Italy into one nation in the middle of the nineteenth century. The Church still exercised control over the Papal States that divided the kingdoms of the north from those of the south on the peninsula. The reunification struggle reached its goal with the invasion of the Papal States and the capture of Rome in 1870. Papal resistance to this military conquest fueled anti-clerical attitudes throughout the peninsula.

Meanwhile the Franco-Prussian War (1870–1871) led to the unification of separate German states into one country. Otto von Bismarck then became a dominant figure on the European continent. His policies in Germany led to open conflict (*Kulturkampf*) with the Catholic Church over the control of education and the appointment of bishops. Once again, the Church's resistance became resented and fed anti-clericalism there as well.

The unresolved tensions between France and Germany exploded unexpectedly into a devastating European-wide conflict. World War I (1914–1918) shook the foundations of Europe. This time the struggles were not directly related to religious conflict. The fear of national militancy following this war led to the establishment of the League of Nations.

But in 1917 the Bolsheviks took over control of Russia. Lenin and then Stalin introduced a reign of terror in an effort to enforce Marxism as the ruling ideology. Russia then began to expand its control to neighboring countries to form the Soviet Union. Marxism considered religion to be the opium of the people. As a result, those who tried openly to practice Christianity experienced ruthless persecution.

The Japanese invasion of Manchuria (1931); the attack on China (1937); the attack on Pearl Harbor (1941) coupled with the German invasion of Poland (1939); the formation of the Axis with Italy (1940); the invasion of France (1941); and the bombardment of England (1941) brought the United States into an even larger World War II.

This culminated in the initiation of the nuclear age with the atomic bombing of Hiroshima and Nagasaki.

Human reason had not eliminated armed conflict. In fact, the conflicts became even more devastating. Moreover, these political and military developments shifted the role of the Church to the sidelines in most instances. The Church's efforts to promote reconciliation and peace seemed futile. Moreover, open hostility to the Church prompted many Catholics to privatize their faith in order to experience acceptance or to advance in their careers in life.

Pope Pius IX convoked a Council at the Vatican in 1870 to address the role of the Church in the midst of the challenges of the nineteenth century. The bishops convened long enough to address the role of the pope, but were never able to address the roles of bishops, priests, religious, and laity because of Giuseppe Garibaldi's invasion of Rome in 1870. Pope Pius IX went into voluntary captivity at the Vatican. In the wake of this military threat to the Church, he drew on the unfinished work of the Council to make a solemn definition of the infallibility of the pope. Subsequent popes, deprived of the Papal States, became remarkably more free to attend to the spiritual mission of the Church.

The Second Vatican Council

This is the wider background for the bold initiative of Pope John XXIII in announcing the convening of a Second Vatican Council. The Church was indeed living in a dramatically new era and needed to reexpress her identity and mission in the face of all these challenges. Fortunately, the same France and Germany that suffered all the turmoil described above were also the setting for a remarkable theological renewal. Theologians like Yves Congar (1904–1995), Henri de Lubac (1913–1991), Louis Bouyer (1913–2004), Marie–Dominique Chenu (1895–1990), Hugo Rahner (1900–1968), Karl Rahner (1904–1984), and Hans Urs von Balthasar (1905–1988) became involved in a genuine effort to return to the sources of Sacred Scripture and the patristic tradition to bring new life to the systematic study of the faith. Moreover, men like Eugene Masure, Gustave Thils, Emile Guerry, Joseph Lecuyer, and A. M. Charue were engaged in theological work on the ordained priesthood. Some of these theologians suffered suspicions of modernism for a while. But all of them remained faithful and persevered in providing rich theological resources for the bishops of the Council. Pope Pius XII (1939–1959), a good theologian himself, had already begun to draw on some of this research in his own encyclical letters on the Church (*Mystici Corporis* in 1943) and on the Liturgy (*Mediator Dei* in 1947).

The time of the Council was an exhilarating moment of history to experience. From the very beginning, the Council Fathers resisted the initial membership on the preparatory commissions and the outlines of the first drafts presented to them. The bishops from France, Germany, Belgium, and the Netherlands had brought with them, as consultants, the theologians who had already been engaged in the movement of the *nouvelle theologie* described above. They were to make a significant contribution to the deliberations.

The first session focused primarily on the Liturgy. Thus, the Fathers of the Council initially addressed the worship of God. The text made clear that the Paschal Mystery lay at the heart of Christian Liturgy. The Fathers recognized that the faithful needed to understand better what they were celebrating in sacrament. This called for education and formation. It also allowed for the use of the vernacular if local bishops' conferences requested it. Translation was to reflect the beauty and sublimity of the Latin texts and retain their doctrinal content. Participation in the Liturgy was to be informed, interior, and engaged. This was the principal document treated during the first session.

But before the conclusion of the first session, the Council Fathers reviewed preliminary drafts of a document on the Church and another on revelation. The first was adopted as a working document with many recommended changes. The second did not receive a majority vote in favor. Since the conciliar norms required a two-thirds vote to reject a working draft, the text technically had survived the vote. After the session was completed, Pope John XXIII intervened to rule that there was not sufficient support for the text and to withdraw it from consideration. He expanded membership on the drafting commission and asked for a new draft. Shortly thereafter, John XXIII, who had been battling cancer, died. But his action opened the Council to the beneficial contributions of the European theologians who had been engaged in such important theological work by returning to the sources and engaging the challenges of modern thought.

Vatican II and the Priesthood

The Council's teaching on the priesthood was rather extensive even though there was no doctrinal document dedicated exclusively to it. The third chapter of the 1964 Dogmatic Constitution on the Church (*Lumen Gentium*) and the 1965 Decree on Priestly Life and Ministry (*Presby-terorum Ordinis*)[1] offer significant teaching as well as practical directives.

Lumen Gentium identifies Christ as the primordial priest in the New Covenant.[2] In the Church there is both the priesthood of all the baptized that involves all the People of God[3] and the ministerial priesthood.[4] These ways of participating in the priesthood of Christ are different, not only in degree, but in essence.[5] The ministerial priesthood serves the common priesthood of the faithful, helping people to live out the truth of their calling in Baptism.

The Council affirmed three degrees of Holy Orders: episcopate, priesthood, and diaconate. Each degree shares in a threefold ministry of Word, sacrament, and pastoral charity, but in distinctive ways. The bishop has a special role in ensuring that the ministry of Word, all preaching and teaching, is in fidelity to the revelation handed down in the Church. The priest has a special responsibility to ensure that the faithful on the local scene have access to sacramental life. The deacon has the special focus on the pastoral charity of those in need.

The ordained priest shares in the ministry of the bishop. He offers a ministry of Word[6] when he preaches[7] or teaches in the Church's name.[8] He is a steward of God's grace in sacramental ministry.[9] He shares with his bishop the

[1] *The Documents of Vatican II*, ed. Walter M. Abbot, trans. Joseph Gallagher (St. Louis, MO: Herder and Herder, 1966).

[2] *Lumen Gentium*, no. 3.

[3] Ibid., nos. 9–17.

[4] Ibid., nos. 18–29.

[5] Ibid., no. 10.

[6] Ibid., no. 24.

[7] Ibid., no. 25.

[8] Ibid., no. 21.

[9] Ibid., no. 26.

governance of the Good Shepherd[10] as he helps to lead the faithful to Christian maturity and tries to ensure good order in the exercise of the charisms of the Holy Spirit.

The Council Fathers emphasized strongly that the ordained priest belongs to a presbyterate. His life and ministry is corporate. He is to exercise it in a collegial relationship with his bishop and his fellow priests.

In doing so he is always to remember as well that he is one with all the faithful he serves by virtue of a shared Baptism. The priest, then, is ordained not to dominate the faithful but to serve them, not to be a loner but to be incorporated into a presbyterate.

Some Implications

The conciliar teaching has profound implications for the spirituality that then should imbue the priest's life. *Presbyterorum Ordinis* spells this out. As with the original apostles, discipleship has to come first.[11] Unless the candidate for the priesthood comes to know and dwell with the Lord, he will struggle to make the sacrifice required of good priestly life. He must learn to love the Lord above all and continue to deepen this communion with the Lord as he lives his life as a priest.

Then in ordination, a priest becomes incorporated in the Headship role of Christ in relation to his Body, the Church. In keeping with Gospel teaching, this ministry is in *service* to the faithful, not in dominion over them. The Council also wanted particularly to encourage priests to recognize that the very ministry that they are ordained to fulfill offers a source for priestly spirituality. In order to preach well,

[10] Ibid., no. 27.
[11] *Presbyterorum Ordinis*, no. 12.

immersion in a life of prayerful reflection on the Word of God is indispensable.[12] In order to be engaged appropriately in the celebration of the Eucharist, the priest needs to unite himself interiorly with Christ both priest and victim. If he is to be a good confessor, he needs to be a good penitent. In order to shepherd the flock worthily, the priest needs to enter into the ascetism of self-gift[13] through embracing a spousal love for the Church.[14]

Since the priest is ordained into a corporate reality, he needs to embrace ever more fully his spiritual sonship with his bishop,[15] his spiritual brotherhood with his fellow priests,[16] and his spiritual fatherhood of those entrusted to his care.[17] He does this as a member of a presbyterate in communion with his bishop.[18]

Then living the evangelical virtues with an ever-deepening engagement enables him to offer a spiritual witness to the kingdom of God. Celibacy enables him to live even now a share in the new humanity as he consecrates himself to the Lord and to his Church.[19] Simplicity of life gives tangible witness to the Gospel message that the Christian's permanent home is not here, but hereafter.[20] Obedience keeps any tendency to willfulness in check and assures him that he is fulfilling the will of God in his life.[21]

In this context, it is easier to understand how the spiritual practices that are presented to candidates for the priesthood in seminary formation today are not arbitrary.

[12] Ibid., nos. 4–5.
[13] Ibid., no. 13.
[14] Ibid., no. 16.
[15] Ibid., no. 2.
[16] Ibid., nos. 7–8.
[17] Ibid., no. 6.
[18] Ibid., no. 8.
[19] Ibid., no. 16.
[20] Ibid., no. 17.
[21] Ibid., no. 15.

Rather, they are directed to the inner engagement that is so important if priestly ministry is going to come alive and bear fruit.

Lord Jesus, who modeled for me what it means to lay down your life in priestly self-sacrifice for the salvation and sanctification of your disciples, help me to offer my life in priestly service to the salvation and sanctification of your priestly people. Grant this in your own name. Amen.

Chapter 12

The Implementation of Vatican II: Navigating Choppy Waters

Just as it took over a century for the widespread implementation of the Council of Trent, so the implementation of the Second Vatican Council is still a work in progress. The efforts at implementation were affected as much by developments outside the Church as within.

The Historical Context

In the United States the 1960s were marked by considerable political turmoil. In 1963 President Kennedy was assassinated. Five years later Dr. Martin Luther King Jr. and Robert Kennedy met the same fate. The movement for racial justice brought together many people of good will across racial and religious lines. In 1968 President Johnson signed civil rights legislation, thus providing the legal foundation for eliminating unjust racial discrimination.

At the same time, the United States had become embroiled, first under Kennedy and then under Johnson, in a war to prevent the expansion of Communism in Asia. This war against the Viet Cong was extremely difficult to wage in a land so far away. Casualties began to mount while little progress seemed to be made. Gradually, support for the war began to falter. The American people became seriously divided on the issue. Public dissent became so strong that Lyndon Johnson abandoned his intention to run for a second term.

Meanwhile, the medical discovery of a contraceptive pill ushered in a sexual revolution. Many women now began to think they could become as sexually active as men without running the risk of conceiving a baby. Cultural icons heralded a period of "free love".

The excitement and turmoil of the sixties then gave way to sober soul searching about the identity and mission of the country in the seventies. The Watergate political scandal undermined respect for and trust in authority. The political anguish leading up to the resignation of President Nixon cast a pall over the country. A brief period of hope with the election of President Jimmy Carter soon led to further America's self-doubt with the prolonged Iranian hostage crisis.

The eighties brought a bit more buoyancy with the upbeat personality of President Ronald Reagan. The collapse of Communism in an unbloody way capped this more hopeful decade.

But the great difficulties involved in many countries trying to transition from tyranny to some form of democracy, from Communism to some form of capitalism, have meant that the subsequent decades continued to experience political turmoil. The Arab-Israeli conflict, terrorist activities originating in Afghanistan, expansionist dreams on the part of Iraq, and the militaristic activities of Iran have kept the Mideast in turmoil. Now the aggressive activities of North Korea and China pose significant threats in the East.

Challenges in the Catholic Church

This political and cultural instability impacted the Church. Even while the Second Vatican Council was progressing, two stories began to emerge: one participated in by the Fathers of the Council; the other, the media interpretation of the serious debate of the participants. The first was a story of Council Fathers drawing on the work of theologians and deliberating openly and sometimes contentiously on how best to present with deeper insight and conviction the faith of the Church and her moral teaching to a world becoming more secular and suspicious of religion. The second story, described largely in political terms, played up a tension between liberal and conservative bishops over the direction of the Church. The first story emphasized engagement with the world on revelation's terms. The second story seemed to focus on the engagement of revelation on the world's terms. Then after the conclusion of the Council, theologians began writing about the Council in two different ways: some focused on continuity in doctrine; others, on more of a rupture with the past, opening up new ways for the future. These contrasting interpretations have developed a life of their own, causing polarization in the life of the Church.

These contrasting narratives were reinforced in 1968 with the divided reception to Pope Paul VI's *Humanae Vitae*. This encyclical letter addressed the role of sexual love in marriage and reaffirmed the Church teaching on artificial contraception. Within weeks after the release of the encyclical on July 25, 1968, a significant number of theologians published statements of public dissent. Even some bishops equivocated in their public statements. This sequel to *Humanae Vitae* seemed to deepen the divide among theologians over the larger interpretation of the Second Vatican Council. The division then began to seep into the whole Church as bishops, priests, religious, and lay leaders took sides.

Thus, the secular sexual revolution penetrated the Church. Moral theologians began to raise serious questions about the Church's sexual moral teaching. Some priests and religious began to experiment with sexual activity. Significant numbers left the priesthood and religious life to marry. Married couples who had been experiencing difficulties with each other or the Church's teaching began to experiment as well. With the decline in vocations, more homosexually oriented men were accepted into seminaries. As was learned later on, priests and religious had begun to victimize underage children or youth and vulnerable adults. Some of this activity was fully public at the time. But much of the victimizing of others has only recently become public in the clergy sex abuse scandal revelations. Confidence not only in priests but also in bishops has been undermined because of the sometimes inept way in which these scandals have been handled.

In more recent decades, a hermeneutic of suspicion has begun to pervade a great deal of public discourse. News outlets interpret daily events through ideological prisms. Talk shows and social media have become vehicles for vitriolic attacks. When the spiritual nature of the struggle is ignored, more people seem to engage in cultural or political or cyber warfare. This tends to marginalize the unique message of the Gospel.

Efforts of Renewal

During his papacy, Pope John Paul II made a concerted effort to promote a more unified interpretation of Vatican II. The Extraordinary Synod of Bishops in 1985 explicitly addressed the reception of the Council and chose to emphasize *communion* as the prism to use in studying its teaching and as the hermeneutic for the interpretation of that teaching. The *Catechism of the Catholic Church*, published in 1992, became one of the more important fruits of that synod. John Paul II's encyclical letter *Veritatis Splendor* (1993) addressed fundamental issues in the Church's moral teaching. The previous year (1992), he released the post-synodal apostolic exhortation *Pastores Dabo Vobis*, on priestly life and ministry. This latter document summarized the conciliar teaching on ministerial priesthood and addressed the spirituality that needs to animate the life of a priest.

Pope Benedict XVI, who as Prefect of the Congregation for the Doctrine of the Faith had contributed to the development of his predecessor's teaching, offered indepth insights into the same teaching in his own homilies and talks. Pope Francis has been able to presume this significant body of post-conciliar teaching, as he has helped the Church to focus on the importance of being a joyful witness to this teaching in an evangelizing outreach to those on the peripheries of Church life and human life.

Saints Lead the Way

As Pope Francis continually reminds us, living priestly life in such a way as to provide a joyful witness to Christ and his message offers the most credible approach to take. It is significant that the convener of the Council, Pope

John XXIII; the pope who brought the Council to con-
clusion and guided the early years of its implementation,
Paul VI; and the pope who has offered the most compre-
hensive body of teaching in the wake of the Council, John
Paul II, are now canonized saints (in 2014, 2018, and 2014,
respectively). In our own country, a Redemptorist bishop,
John Neumann, who served in the United States of America, was canonized in 1977. A Redemptorist priest, Francis
Xavier Seelos, was beatified in 2000; a Capuchin priest,
Solanus Casey, and a diocesan priest, Stanley Rother, both
in 2017. Archbishop Fulton Sheen is expected to be beatified soon. Many other priests and bishops throughout the
world have also been similarly recognized. It is in the lives
of these men that we best see the recipe for holiness of life.
Each brought a unique personality and set of gifts to the
responsibilities entrusted to them. Each evidenced heroic
charity in the way in which they fulfilled their ministry.
Each manifested a personal communion with the Lord
through prayer. Each brought an apostolic zeal for the
redemptive and sanctifying mission of the Lord to their
activities. Saints are the priests who point the way for the
renewal of the priesthood.

*Lord Jesus, who reveal to us in the Church your saving and sanc-
tifying love, help me even in turbulent times to be the vehicle of
that love that you call me to be and to express it in a truly Gospel
way of life. All this I ask in your own name. Amen.*

Chapter 13

Lessons from History
for a Renewed Priesthood

History then teaches us that in every period, the Church has faced challenges, large or small. She has had to seek new ways of remaining true to her original mission while adjusting to new circumstances. Like a human organism, the Body of Christ has had significant growing pains. Sometimes disease has taken hold and seemingly threatened her continued life. Healing has not always come easily. But Christ promised to be with her until the end of time (Mt 28:20).

In addressing the significant challenges that the Church faces today, it is important to keep this historical perspective in mind. The scandals arising from clergy sex abuse, financial mismanagement, and episcopal failures are horrendous. The issues that the wider society presents to faith and moral living are huge. But the Church has been through daunting difficulties in the past. And the Lord has remained faithful. The ordained priesthood in the Church, to whom the Lord entrusted his Church in a special way (Mt 28:16–20), has had to undergo repeated purifications in order to reappropriate the Lord's original mandate.

Sacred Scripture

The priest, by virtue of the sacramental seal, is configured into Christ's unique relationship to his Father through the Holy Spirit. Thus, he shares in a special way in the Lord's redemptive mission and the Holy Spirit's sanctifying mission, expressed in a threefold ministry of Word, sacrament, and pastoral care. But priests carry this sacred role in earthen vessels (2 Cor 4:7). They have the awesome responsibility to serve in Christ's name as Head of his Body, Shepherd of his flock, and Spouse of his Bride. Priests have been often quite flawed vessels! Some, like Simon Peter, have been able to repent, experience forgiveness, and reembrace their mission fruitfully. Others, like Judas, have suffered tragic ends. It is a mystery that Christ has chosen to continue his saving mission in the world through such imperfect men.

The New Testament is not silent about the weaknesses of the first apostles. Mostly illiterate, bumbling in their comprehension of his words and actions, beset by rivalry for special privileges, cowardly in the face of Jesus' arrest, torture, and execution, these same men (except Judas) eventually became living instruments of the Holy Spirit in reaching the ends of the earth with the Gospel of the Lord, and they laid down their lives in testimony to him and his Gospel.

The Period of the Early Persecutions

As Ignatius of Antioch attested, the early successors to the apostles experienced the full virulence of violent persecution. Some succumbed and betrayed their Master and mission. Others, like Ignatius, evidenced remarkable courage and conviction as they willingly embraced martyrdom. They were unafraid to become victims offered in sacrifice as priests, in union with the Lord. In fact, it was the martyrdom of these early witnesses that gave credibility to their message. The death of martyrs became the seed of Christians.[1]

Priestly Life after the Persecutions

A different challenge emerged when organized persecution ceased with Constantine's Edict of Milan. Priests and laity both began to accommodate to the worldly culture. This led to mediocrity in Christian living. Genuine disciples had to reach more deeply to find the best way to live the Gospel life. St. John Chrysostom became an articulate voice, calling priests to take the spiritual struggle to heart. He was convinced that the Church needed priestly spiritual warriors if the faithful were going to see the importance of engaging in this warfare themselves. He did not mince words in taking priests to task when they hesitated in this mission.

While John Chrysostom, coming out of the desert experience, presented this challenge in the Christian East,

[1] See Tertullian, *Apologetics*, trans. Rudolph Arbermann, Emily Joseph Daly, C.S.J., and Edwin Quain, S.F. (New York: Fathers of the Church, 1950), Chap. 48.

St. Augustine took on this issue in the West. Augustine knew through painful personal experience how easy it is to accommodate to a fallen world. He also knew the difference that a priest like Ambrose of Milan could make. Augustine framed the discipleship that priests needed to embrace as a choice between furthering the city of God or surrendering to the city of man. The priest, and the people with him, must make a fundamental choice between living for God or living for self; for self-gift or self-centeredness. Each of these witnesses, John Chrysostom and Augustine, recognized the subtle and seductive attraction of a false accommodation to the world in the form of a socially acceptable Christianity. They recognized and fought clerical privilege as the enemy of Gospel discipleship. According to them, the ordained need to lead and serve by taking the Gospel challenge to worldly accommodation very seriously.

The Feudal Experience

The Church in subsequent centuries became more and more immersed in ordinary life in the civilized world. The Church also became the great civilizer of the marauding tribes from the northern parts of Europe, engaging in a remarkably fruitful missionary effort. But again the great danger was inappropriate accommodation in order to make Christianity more attractive. St. Gregory the Great became an astute observer of this challenge and urged careful discernment. Missionaries need to identify the seeds of the Gospel in the peoples they are evangelizing, but also be alert to the seeds of the enemy. Thus, Gregory urged the "art of arts" to discern how to encourage the good and resist the bad. Those who followed his counsel became great apostolic missionaries. Those who did not compromised the Gospel message.

The feudal social structure presented its own challenges. Bishops, abbots, and pastors often exercised civil administrative responsibilities along with ecclesial governance. The lines between church and state sometimes became quite blurred. Some priests became so immersed in temporal governance that they lost their way. Pope Eugene III, who had moved from serving as the Cistercian Abbot of San Andrea near Rome to being elected as pope, found himself bewildered by the expectations of the people. He was not only the Bishop of Rome but also the governor of the Papal States. St. Bernard of Clairvaux responded to his fellow Cistercian's plea for help by urging him to focus on spiritual fatherhood. Every father has some administrative responsibilities for his family, but the spiritual dimensions of his fatherhood have to be primary. Bernard insisted that the pope needed to handle many administrative chores through the selection of and delegation to good collaborators. Then he would be free to fulfill what was primary in his mission: the salvation and sanctification of those entrusted to his care. Pope Eugene responded. But other bishops and priests failed the Church by allowing temporal responsibilities to eclipse the spiritual ones and often succumbing to the temptations of a fallen world: arrogance, greed, and lust.

The High Middle Ages

The height of the Middle Ages presented a new set of challenges. Religious piety was flourishing, but informed understanding and living of the faith was floundering. The faithful were enthralled with the building of magnificent Gothic cathedrals. They were inspired by the Divine Presence in the Eucharist. But priests were not experiencing good preparation for ordination. Many had little or no theological formation. They were sometimes ordained as "Mass priests" who celebrated the Holy Sacrifice of the Mass but without the training or authority to preach, teach, or counsel. St. Thomas Aquinas tried to bring to this challenging situation a serious commitment of study, prayer, and the living of the evangelical life. He, too, shared a deep devotion to the Eucharist, but wanted priests to grow in learning the depth and breadth of the mystery presented in the sacrament of the altar. He promoted serious study of philosophy and theology as well as a healthy appreciation for the physical sciences in order to help candidates for the priesthood to grapple with the substance of the faith in their lives. He was convinced that prayer and evangelical witness had to accompany this effort.

Reform: Protestant and Catholic

Unfortunately, the Church struggled to hear that message. University study suffered from political and ideological squabbles. The life of bishops and priests continued to exhibit moral decadence. Devotional life became the most important resource for keeping the faith alive among the laity. This was the situation that prompted Martin Luther to recognize the desperate need for reform in the Church and in the priesthood. His focus on grace, faith, Sacred Scripture, and good preaching was very important in a Church that had accommodated too much to a decadent worldly culture. But unfortunately, he did not remain within the fold as he tended to absolutize his insights at the expense of *human cooperation* with grace, the need for *works* to accompany faith, the role of *Sacred Tradition* and the *ecclesial Magisterium* in the interpretation of Scripture, and the gift of *sacrament* as the realized expression of the mysteries of faith. So it was necessary for the Council of Trent to launch a

Catholic Reformation that reunited God's role with man's; faith with works; Sacred Scripture with Sacred Tradition and Magisterium; the ministry of Word with the ministry of sacrament; Gospel discipleship with ordained apostleship.

A Catholic Renewal

Post-conciliar France was convulsed by the wars of religion. Politics and religion became intertwined. The royalty sided with the Catholics, and the nobles with the Protestants. Priests often got caught in the crossfire. In this atmosphere, the French School of Spirituality took the teaching of the Council of Trent seriously—but recognized that the renewal needed was not only doctrinal or even disciplinary but truly spiritual. Discipleship required deep immersion in *the one* Mystery of Faith that embraced all the mysteries of faith on a more profound level. Only if the priest is plunged into this central, unifying, and transforming mystery in the depths of his being, will he become a good disciple of the Lord and help the faithful to do so as well. A priest's awareness of this reassures him in his identity in relation to the Triune God and his mission to the redemptive mystery for others. He is to become a priest-victim, one who offers himself in sacrifice along with the Lord. Thus, the priest could reclaim his unique role in the midst of the political-religious conflicts.

Vatican Council II

The Second Vatican Council was convened after the revolutions in America, France, and Russia and two world wars. The world sought a new vision and new hope. The Council Fathers appreciated this and wanted to move the Church to a positive dialogue with the world. In a society that had become anti-clerical, the Council sought to restore emphasis on service in the discipleship of the priest. The priest's whole existence is for service to the redemptive mission of the Lord and the sanctifying mission of the Holy Spirit. The very demands of his ministry of Word, sacrament, and pastoral care should help him realize that good discipleship requires interior engagement rather than the mere external fulfillment of these responsibilities in themselves. His is a vocation, not a career. The evangelical virtues are intended to help him witness to the Gospel by his very way of life. His ministry was to be directed to the real life issues people face and the social issues that often undergird them.

But the Council's vision sometimes got lost in the turbulence that followed. The organic development envisioned by the Council became undermined by the convulsions in society at large and the varied interpretations of the teachings of the Council within the Church. This turmoil sometimes undermined confidence and conviction in the priesthood. The departures of priests from priestly ministry and religious from consecrated life, disagreements over the interpretation of conciliar teaching, and dissent regarding sexual morality created an atmosphere where the vibrancy of Catholic faith began to wane. This is the historical background for addressing the needed spiritual renewal in the Church today.

Lord Jesus, who are ever faithful to your Church through her experience of sin and virtue, conflict and reconciliation, scandal and holiness, help me to experience that conversion of heart as well as growth in virtue and holiness of life that will enable me to be the priest you want me to be for your people. Grant this in your own name. Amen.

Chapter 14

A Renewed Church Radiating the Love of the Lord

Today's Reality

Yes, the Church is sinful and holy. Bishops and priests have been both scoundrels and saints. The same is true today. So, what is the renewal that the Church needs in our own time?

Simply stated, the Church needs God! The Church needs to seek God, kneel in adoration before God, love God above all, and become more fully an icon of God's presence to the world. God is ever present, active, offering himself in saving and sanctifying love. To receive and then mirror that presence, the Church, like Mary, has to be open, receptive, and responsive to God's divine overture of self-gift. His pursuit of his people is indeed an overture, a musical dance of love, using every movement available to invite them to accept his embrace.

Yes, the whole Bible is a revelation of the persistent ways in which God has offered himself in human history as their Maker and Redeemer earnestly desiring to enter a spousal union with his people. The whole drama of human existence reveals God's repeated offer and his people's ambivalent response.

As so often in the past, God seems to be inviting his wayward Spouse into desert suffering to persuade her anew (cf. Hos 2:16). Once again, he seems to be inviting a holy encounter that begins with the experience of God's pursuing love, leads to repentant love, acknowledges humbly the need to be saved and sanctified, and culminates in a transformed, elevated way of living Gospel life. Yes, the Church needs to fall in love with the Lord!

The Church will come alive when she vibrates with the love of the Lord. God has given to his Church the pearl of great price. He now calls her to give up all that stands in the way in order to reappropriate it (Mt 13:45–46). This is a time to look forward with a confidence born of Gospel living. Whenever scandal has rocked the Church, God has raised up remarkable men and women to model what it means to take the Gospel seriously and become men and women truly in love with the Lord.

The Challenges

The challenges are real. The leakage in the Church is alarming. One-third of baptized Catholics living today in the United States no longer consider themselves Catholic. That percentage approaches one half if we focus on those born in the last thirty years. Some studies report that young people now begin drifting away at the average age of thirteen. Overall, only a quarter of Catholics participate with some degree of regularity in Sunday Mass. Obviously, a merely cultural Catholicism will no longer support the faith. The baptized need to be helped to meet the Lord in a truly life-changing way and then to continue deepening that relationship with the Lord in his Church.

When surveyed, Catholics who have left the Church identify a number of issues: loss of belief in the Christian narrative; the seeming irrelevance of the Mass and other sacraments; the busyness of their lives; the impression that the Church is anti-woman or too much of a male-dominated institution; the difficulty of reconciling a loving God with the prevalence of so much evil or of reconciling the Bible with the discoveries of science; the perceived irrelevance of the Church's sexual moral teaching.

A significant obstacle to meeting God in the present culture is the superficiality that addiction to digital media can cause. Preoccupation with the latest posting, commercial, enticing image, or electronic game can lead people into incessant distraction. Then any compulsion to gratify the senses can trap unsuspecting participants into an ever-increasing need to explore, experiment, and then surrender to seductive stimulations. When this happens, people live on the surface of life and lose the capacity for more in-depth recollection and reflection.

Underneath all of these reasons seems to be an ever more pervasive disappointment in not experiencing God in the Church. Even though God is there offering himself, more people experience difficulty in finding him there, often because they fail to see him in their priests. As a result, an unhappy world seems to be looking desperately for every possible avenue to a happiness that only God can provide and in every possible place save the one through which God most wants to make himself available.

Response

The challenging issues raised by so many require intelligent and loving engagement. It is important to be ready to give a reason for Christian hope (cf. 1 Pet 3:16). The Church needs a new apologetics that is not polemical but addresses the questions raised by those who have moved to the fringes of faith by offering insight, knowledge, and pastoral love. It is important to listen first to the life stories of each in order to know where to begin to join them in their spiritual journey. Those who consider the faith outdated or irrelevant are not necessarily hostile to faith. Many have just drifted away. Engaged in the right way, they often reveal themselves to be open, even inquisitive. So, the Church has to be willing to listen, to treat each person with respect, to exhibit appreciation for each person's journey, and then to be unafraid to engage them about the way the truths of faith speak to their real life experience.

But the ultimate issue is God. Is he real? Why does the relentless pursuit of the good things this world offers not satisfy? It is intriguing that a gradually increasing number of millennials are on a spiritual quest. They often find life to be too stressful and empty. Yes, the Church has to be ready to address every honest intellectual question with insight and persuasion. Ultimately, however, people, whether they realize it or not, are seeking an *encounter* with the Divine.

The Church has a role in inviting people into deeper quiet. It is very difficult to address the more important questions in life without nurturing sufficient interior silence. Sacred Scripture reminds people that God speaks more clearly in sustained quiet.

Sometimes the experience of uplifting beauty in creation or in awe-inspiring art, architecture, music, or poetry can touch the deeper recesses of the soul and open the heart to God. When Notre Dame Cathedral in Paris was being ravaged by fire, some people expressed memories of awe experienced during their visits there in the past. As the fire raged, Charles Lewis, a Canadian journalist, penned a blog entry entitled "I Worshipped the Goddess of Reason— Until I Met the God of Mercy in Notre Dame".[1] In this blog he recounted how, as a young secular tourist, he visited the cathedral and marveled at the architecture and the art. Then he spied a young woman making her confession in an open confessional. Something spoke to his heart. He could not erase that moving image from his memory. God used that scene to invite him to faith. Eventually, he embraced the Catholic faith, repented of his past life, and moved forward to a new life with direction and purpose. God can knock at the door of the human heart in countless ways!

A Sinful Church

Unfortunately, the Church today faces a huge self-inflicted wound: the clergy sex abuse scandal has created a moral disaster. It has tragically undermined the credibility of the ordained messenger. In a world wherein the Church's sexual teaching seems ridiculous to many and the preachers of that message have failed miserably in living that teaching, the victims are not only those physically abused but all who find themselves confused, demoralized, or betrayed by those who were supposed to be bearing witness to life-giving truth. Bishops, too, have failed them. How many are hurt! How many are bewildered, angered, and cast adrift!

The Church is indeed embracing reform measures to heal the harmed and to restore trust. Pope Francis' February 2019 summit with the presidents of all the bishops'

[1] Charles Lewis, "I Worshipped the Goddess of Reason—Until I Met the God of Mercy at Notre Dame" (blog), *National Catholic Register*, April 15, 2019.

conferences in the world and his subsequent motu proprio *Vos Estis Lux Mundi*, incorporating new universal laws
governing the Church's response, have pointed the way
to structural reform. With his Apostolic Constitution *Pascite gregem Dei*, Pope Francis has now revised Book VI of
the Code of Canon Law to incorporate these disciplinary
and penal measures.[2] The 2019 Baltimore meetings of the
United States Conference of Catholic Bishops (USCCB)
have built substantively on the USCCB Dallas Charter of
2002, focused on priests, and the 2019 papal norms, including bishops, so as to provide even more specific measures: an independent third-party reporting mechanism for
reporting serious concerns about bishops; an ecclesiastical
structure, with significant lay participation, for handling,
examining, and assessing the validity of allegations; and a
series of canonical measures for the restriction of the ministry of any bishop credibly accused.

Holiness of Life

But the ultimate antidote to scandal has to be holiness of
life. Disciplinary reform offers an ecclesiastical structure
for the body. Spiritual renewal addresses the soul. The
United States Conference of Catholic Bishops has adopted
a *Code of Conduct for Bishops* to expand and supplement the
previous code for priests adapted in 2002. But an explicit
commitment to pursue holiness of life is an indispensable
condition for the baptized and especially for those ordained
or aspiring to ordination.

The deepest desire in the human person is for that happiness that God alone can offer. As Augustine testified, "Our
hearts are made for you, O God, and they will not rest

---

[2] Francis, Apostolic Constitution *Pascite gregum Dei* (June 1, 2021).

until they rest in you."[3] Augustine did not come to this realization easily. It took more than thirty years of life! He had to experience a series of disappointments and dead-ends before allowing himself to be grasped by the only love that can satisfy: God himself.

God is always trying to offer himself. But people can build all sorts of defenses. Not all the difficulties are external! How important it is, then, to uncover and awaken the deepest interior desire that God has planted in each human soul. That desire, come alive and nurtured, renders the human person less defensive and more receptive to what God wants to give most: himself. Those drawn to God mention unique ways in which God has "spoken" to their hearts. Usually, this speaking is not an explicit word, but an unmistakable tug of the heart. Sometimes it happens in a moment of quiet in which all the alternate attractions of the world seem to slip into secondary relevance.

God can even use a growing disgust with the pursuit of self-gratification, self-promotion, and worldly success as an opening to get a hearing. Evidence is mounting that more millennials are becoming disenchanted with the pressured pursuit of what the world considers achievement and accomplishment. Inner peace and joy are an attractive alternative to stress and loneliness. God can use any experience or event to win attention.

The Spiritual Struggle

God usually offers a sense of relief when he finally receives a hearing. He wants to invite response with the offer of his saving love. But the journey in response to this love soon

[3] Augustine, *Confessions* I, 1, trans. John Ryan (New York: Doubleday Image, 1960).

meets obstacles. Desires that compete with God soon rear their ugly head. To tame them so that they do not suffocate that deeper desire for God involves a spiritual battle. This can seem daunting. Some will lose heart.

St. John Chrysostom addressed that struggle in quite realistic terms. The capital vices (or sins) are still deadly! It takes a warrior to be willing to engage in the ascetical effort that is required. This effort is really about experiencing greater spiritual freedom. The more untamed desires rule people, the more enslaved they are; the more these competing desires are tamed, the more people become inwardly free. Each "no" to an enslaving desire is a "yes" to greater spiritual freedom. Pride must gradually yield to humility; envy to a greater appreciation of one's own unique call in life; greed to stewardship and magnanimity; anger to strong love; lust to chaste love; gluttony to temperate eating and drinking; sloth to spiritual initiative and zeal. Only God can make this journey possible by his grace. The journey in this life is always slow, gradual, and partial.

This battle, Augustine taught, is a personal struggle in service to a greater common good. The disciple early on faces a fundamental choice between self-centeredness and God-centeredness. The response has not only personal implications but also social consequences. Is it going to be the city of man or the city of God?

A Dark Night

The cloud hovering over the Church today seems to cast a heavy shadow over this journey to the city of God. The Church is wounded by serious sin. This has driven some away and disillusioned many others. But the sun shines beyond and even through the cloud. Has God allowed such grievous sin to grip his Church in order to purify her of some false accommodations to the world? Does God want to raise up members of his Church who are willing to engage in an ascetical struggle for her moral and spiritual renewal?

When the Church was in disarray at the time of the Protestant Reformation, St. John of the Cross offered his perceptive teaching on the *dark night*. The active dark night is the ascetical effort described in the struggle against the capital vices. But he also recognized that a passive dark night is a moment of grace. When life is tranquil, God seems close. When life is dark and turbulent, he seems absent. But the truth is that God is present in both situations. The difference is *feeling* his presence in one and not *feeling* his presence in the second. So, Christians need to be skeptical about equating objective reality with personal feeling. The truth is that God is always present, offering delights (dessert) in times of consolation, but substantive food (the main course) in the times of desolation.[4] In effect, God uses the "night experience" to open up interior space and time for him to enter and offer a true and deeper light or "day experience" in the lives of his disciples.

There is no question that the Church has a serious responsibility to reach out in compassionate healing to the victims of sex abuse, to their family members and loved ones also impacted, and to the significant numbers of people who feel betrayed, disillusioned, angry, and sad. This outreach needs to continue to take place in the spirit of the Good Samaritan (Jesus), who reached out to the seriously wounded (all victims) with oil and wine (symbols of the sacraments) and brought him to the inn (the Church) at no

[4] See John of the Cross, *The Dark Night*, in *The Collected Works of St. John of the Cross*, trans. Kieran Kavanaugh, O.C.D., and Otilio Rodriguez, O.C.D. (Washington, DC: Institute of Carmelite Studies, 1973).

further cost to the victim (salvation and healing are free). This Gospel spirit must animate the enhanced structural reforms that the Church has now adopted to complement the earlier reform measures of 2002.

But the deeper challenge involves an interior embrace of the *dark night*. God, in this darkness, is knocking at the door of Christian hearts (Rev 3:20). He wants to enter, but he respects the freedom of each person. He wants the door opened from the inside. In a sense, God seems to be asking, Are there souls who trust enough my Word, my promise, my faithfulness? He offers himself anew as Bridegroom to his Bride, the Church. It will take a purified faith to recognize this and to open the door to him. Are there souls today willing to be victims of love, God's love for the sake of his Church? God has wooed his Church into the desert to speak to her heart words of love. He offers himself anew to purify, transform, and elevate those open to his grace.

This acceptance of the *dark night* as an invitation to experience God in a new, purifying, and transforming way demands not only faith but also hope. Hope is grounded in a blessed conviction that God is acting now and offering a share in his victory over sin, suffering, and death. There is far more benefit in affirming God's presence and cooperating with his grace in the present moment than allowing oneself to be trapped in the hurts of the past or paralyzed by fears about the future. God is offering himself now! Hope clings to that conviction and acts on it.

At the heart of the *dark night* is the invitation to self-giving love. God wants to create space in the human heart for him by depriving the soul of lesser satisfactions that have regularly sustained it in the past. This is uncomfortable but purifying for the soul, making it more possible to receive and give transforming love. This is the only kind of love that frees us for a genuine love of others. The early Church attracted followers because this kind of love was so striking: "Look, how those Christians love one another."

If the Church can raise up souls who are willing to witness to this way of embracing the darkness, then the way to light will be assured. Tragedy can either prompt people to seek worldly solace and relief or open the door to God's saving, sanctifying, and elevating action. The Church needs saints who witness to the way, the truth, and the life! Saintly priests will become attractive witnesses.

Lord Jesus Christ, who offer yourself to me in profound self-gift, grant me the grace in the midst of pain and sorrow to welcome your purifying love in both light and darkness so that I may make an ever fuller gift of myself in response to you. Grant this in your own name. Amen.

Chapter 15

Renewed Priests Embracing the Gospel

What will be the sign to seekers that the Church is truly radiating God and has entered into this spiritual, purifying renewal? The witness of Gospel living in the Church! Real communion with God is expressed in virtue. When more and more people experience the Church living Gospel truth and witnessing to Gospel life, they will not only be more likely to give the Church another look but even be attracted to her.

False Accommodation of the Gospel

Ross Douthat has written a book, *Bad Religion*,[1] which identifies some significant ways in which the Christian

---

[1] Ross Douthat, *Bad Religion* (New York: Free Press of Simon and Schuster, 2012).

churches in the Western world have inappropriately accommodated to the culture in the last half century. For instance, when the Bible is interpreted either with an exclusively historical/scientific methodology on the one hand or in a basically fundamentalist way on the other, the living power of the Word of God suffers. When worship becomes self-expression rather than self-surrender, the right relationship with God is compromised. When the Gospel challenge to accumulating wealth is ignored or a prosperity Gospel promoted, then the Gospel attitude toward the goods of this world can be lost. When the Bible message on sexual morality is interpreted in the light of contemporary sexual behavior rather than current behavior addressed in light of the biblical teaching, then the truth of the Gospel is undermined. When a biblical text is co-opted to promote an ideological Gospel, whether conservative or liberal, the integrity of the scriptural message is easily compromised.

The Evangelical Virtues

The Church has traditionally presented the reliable keys to interpreting and living the Gospel: the three virtues of poverty, chastity, and obedience. They address the distinctive Gospel way to relate to possessions, other people, and ourselves, if Christ is going to be experienced as the Way, the Truth, and the Life (Jn 14:6). When the early persecutions challenged Christians to live Gospel life more radically, commitment to these virtues became an implicit response. The Desert Fathers named them more explicitly. Monks and then apostolic religious communities expressed them in vows. Gradually, the Church invited all the faithful to adopt and adapt them to the responsibilities of their state in life. Why? These virtues address the most powerful human drives, channeling them into support of Gospel living. For this reason they are called the evangelical virtues.

Poverty resists greed by moving the Christian from a tendency to seek security in what the material world has to offer toward a greater simplicity of life and a responsible stewardship of the gifts available in this world. Chastity resists lust by moving the Christian from a tendency to self-gratification toward a greater capacity for self-gift to God and other people. Obedience resists pride by moving the Christian from a tendency to seek ego-control of life toward the embrace of God's will as reflected in one's vocational responsibilities of life, the directives of legitimate superiors, and the concrete challenges of daily living.

While these virtues are significant for all who seek to take seriously the Christian spiritual life, they are particularly important for the ordained. For unless the ordained are living them, they will not be able to preach the fullness of the Gospel message credibly. They may even be inclined to ignore these virtues in their preaching because they are ignoring them in their lives. People do not expect perfection. But they do look for concrete evidence that the ordained man is practicing what the Gospel teaches. This is an indispensable condition for restoring trust in both bishops and priests.

Gospel Simplicity of Life

The Lord Jesus insisted on detachment from riches as a criterion for discipleship. He declared the poor in spirit to be blessed (Mt 5:3). He did not want his disciples to store up treasures on earth lest they ensnare the heart (Mt 6:19–21).

They were forbidden to serve both God and money (Mt 6:24). They were to trust more in God's providential care so that their primary concern could be for his kingdom (Mt 6:25–34). The Lord's strongest statements appear in the parable of the rich man and Lazarus (Lk 16:19–31) and the invitation to the rich young man to sell all, give to the poor, and follow him (Mk 10:21–22). Can there be any doubt about the intent of the Lord's teaching? Ignore this and the Gospel foundation crumbles!

Gospel simplicity of life presents a special challenge in an affluent culture. Is God nudging the Church into dispossession in response to the clergy sex abuse crisis? St. Paul wisely admonished Bishop Timothy that covetousness is the root of all evil (1 Tim 6:10–12). Why is that? Is it not because unbridled greed grounds people in this world's values and goals at the expense of God's? How often an opulent clergy lifestyle has led the Church into false accommodations with the fallen world! Simplicity of life is a powerful way to profess authentic detachment from this world's values and to witness to the truth of the Gospel message.

Moreover, simplicity of life is the most credible way to engage in efforts of social justice. Ever since Pope Leo XIII's *Rerum Novarum* (1891) the Church has been developing a rather impressive body of teaching, rooted in Sacred Scripture and Holy Tradition, but applied to the rapidly changing social situations.[2] This teaching has focused on the dignity of every human life, the unique nature and role of the family, human rights and responsibilities, the dignity of human work and the rights of the worker, solidarity with the most needy and vulnerable,

[2] Pontifical Council for Justice and Peace, *Compendium of the Social Doctrine of the Church* (Vatican City State: Libreria Editrice Vaticana, 2004).

subsidiarity in addressing human needs, and stewardship of God's creation. This teaching is intended to promote God's justice: not a worldly utopia, but a "kingdom of truth and life, a kingdom of holiness and grace, a kingdom of justice, love and peace".[3]

The Church does not make a specific requirement of the man being ordained a diocesan priest in this regard. But each priest has already received a mandate to care for those in need in his ordination to the diaconate. Programs of outreach may appropriately be delegated to others. But the bishop or parish priest cannot exempt himself from some personal engagement with the poor. There is no substitute for concrete service to those in need. This is why Pope Francis urges every priest and bishop to go to the peripheries of Church life to meet Christ there.

Moreover, bishops and priests need to exhibit a holy detachment from unnecessary possessions. Obviously, some possessions are necessary for the fulfillment of the responsibilities of office. But luxury should have no place in his life. There is an art to living simply in clothes, taste, hobbies, and vacations. It takes self-discipline to resist the seductions of the products of technology and so experience the needed silence. The goal is to accept those gifts that enhance priestly ministry while forgoing those that stand in the way. Above all, the priest needs to refuse "privilege" lest he begin to expect special treatment. Narcissism in a priest becomes clericalism. Nothing is a greater obstacle to his witness to the kingdom than clericalism. Christ's apostles are to travel lightly in this world in order to give credibility to their preaching about the next. They are to serve others rather than expect others to serve them.

---

[3] Preface for the Solemnity of Jesus Christ, King of the Universe.

In the call to care for those in need, the Church insists that the greatest need people experience is spiritual. Hence, the priest's special mission is to those who are spiritually poor.[4]

Gospel Celibacy

While Gospel simplicity of life addresses the relationship with material possessions, Gospel celibacy addresses the relationship with other people, and ultimately with God. In fact, human sexuality impacts the whole way in which people experience the world. Despite contemporary gender theorists, men and women experience each other and the world in distinctive ways. There are indeed shades of variation, probably influenced by genetic factors and by social rearing that can introduce some ambiguity in this area. But human sexuality invites people into relationships that foster communion.

The more fundamental issue for both men and women is the decision whether to live according to the flesh or according to the spirit (cf. Gal 5:13–26). When St. Paul addresses this challenge, he is not suggesting a dichotomy between the body and the soul. Rather, he speaks of the difference it makes when both body and soul are subject to the Holy Spirit rather than subject to the worldly spirit and the Evil One. The first leads to virtue, the latter to vice. "Do you not know that your body is a temple of the Holy Spirit within you, which you have from God? You are not your own; you were bought with a price. So glorify God in your body" (1 Cor 6:19–20). Paul understood that the whole person had become a new creation

---

[4] See Francis, *Evangelii Gaudium* (November 24, 2013), nos. 197–201.

in Christ and that Christian sexual morality flows from this profound and liberating truth. Thus, he labels sexual immorality as prostituting Christ's body (1 Cor 6:15) and failing to appreciate what Christians have become in faith (1 Cor 6:19–20).

The New Testament witnesses to the special value Jesus placed on celibate life and love. Jesus lifted it up as providing special witness to the kingdom of God (Mt 19:11–12). St. Paul experienced it as freeing him for an undivided gift of himself to Christ for apostolic ministry (1 Cor 7:29–35). The Lord Jesus lived celibately himself, freeing him for a unique intimacy with his Father and for a spousal commitment to the people he served in public ministry.

The evangelical call to celibacy for priests, then, points to a profound relationship first of all to the Lord and then to God's people. Celibacy can never be reduced to a mere canonical requirement for ordination in the Latin Church. To think of it as merely a law that can be dispensed (as already realized in the case of some married former Anglican priests and proposed in the Pan-Amazon Synod) or even abrogated in a future council or by a future pope is to miss the rich spiritual insight and tradition behind its gradual adoption, first in apostolic times and then in local synods or councils—Elvira in Spain (310), Africa (390), Carthage (419)—and finally in the Fourth Lateran Council of 1215. From the early Church, celibacy became an especially respected way of loving the Lord. It was a form of discipleship that freed the person to be more concerned about the realities that relate to the Lord (1 Cor 7:29–35). Celibacy also is a powerful witness in a secular world to the reality of the life to come (Mt 19:11–12). Most of all, celibacy was and is a way of love. As Augustine learned the hard way, self-gift, not self-love, has to characterize discipleship of the Lord. There is nothing more unlovable than an unloving bachelor. There is something mysteriously attractive and inspiring about a priest whose celibate love of the Lord radiates his life and ministry.

Moreover, St. Bernard of Clairvaux has drawn attention to the richness of spiritual paternity to which the celibate bishop and priest are called. After the candidate has consecrated himself in celibate love to the Lord in diaconal ordination, Christ then invites him in priestly ordination into a share in the Lord's spousal love for his Church and paternal love for his adopted sons and daughters. This involves a very spiritual but real way of loving and being loved in the fulfillment of ordained ministry.

Gospel celibacy is also linked to simplicity of life. A bishop or priest ordinarily does not have responsibility for the personal support of others, even though he may have that temporarily for aging parents. This freedom makes it far less necessary to accumulate savings for long-term support. He can, then, be generous in reaching out to support others. In fact, he needs to be vigilant in shunning any temptation to compensate for his sacrifice in celibate love by accumulating worldly possessions or resources. Self-serving love feeds that narcissism which in the ordained takes the form of clericalism. Self-giving love frees the ordained for a pastoral zeal for the salvation and sanctification of the people they serve. The evangelical virtues are closely interrelated.

Gospel Obedience

From the beginning of his earthly life, the Son of God was obedient. He embraced the will of his Father (Heb 10:5–7). Jesus' spirituality found its nourishment in doing the Father's will (Jn 4:34). This desire to seek and fulfill his Father's will became especially expressed in his readiness to hand himself over to the Father (Lk 23:46).

Jesus also enjoined his disciples to do the Father's will. He taught them to pray: "Thy will be done, On earth as it is in heaven" (Mt 6:10). And he stated that any true relationship with him depended on doing the Father's will (Mt 12:50).

This requirement of obedience on the part of subjects includes also correlative obligations on the part of superiors. Those in Holy Orders are to be servants of all (Mk 10:43–45). Shepherds of God's flock are to watch over them "not by constraint but willingly, not for shameful gain but eagerly, not as domineering over those in your charge but being examples to the flock" (1 Pet 5:2–3).

Christian obedience cannot be reduced to a merely juridic reality. It touches the whole relationship that the Christian experiences with God and those who are appointed in the Church to interpret God's will. It is intimately related to faith. Since life is a gift from God, the Christian wishes to listen (ob-audire) to the heart of God to discover his own purpose and destiny. Thus, listening to God with the intent of doing what is heard is the soul of obedience. God manifests his will in creation, in redemption, in his Church, and in the concrete responsibilities connected with one's state in life.

Thus, obedience presumes communion with the heart of Jesus, who lived out his earthly life in communion with his Father. So, it is rooted in faith that God wants each one's happiness. It is sustained by hope that God will accomplish his purpose, even if that purpose is not readily appreciated at the time. It is an expression of love for God that fosters not only communion with him but communion with his Church.

Gospel obedience, most importantly, counteracts self-will. Ever since the rebellion of Adam and Eve, their descendants have inherited a rebellious streak. In a very real way life is marked by a conflict of wills: mankind against God; men against one another. Obedience addresses that fundamental choice which Augustine highlighted. Which is to prevail—the city of God or the city of man? Those who live Gospel obedience choose the city of God!

On the day of ordination, the candidate for ordination places his hands between those of his ordaining bishop. The bishop then asks the candidate if he is willing to promise his Ordinary obedience and respect. When the affirmative response is given, the bishop says: "May God who began the good work in you bring it to fulfillment."

What is the nature of obedience? It is grounded in *sacramental* reality. A man is called by God through the Church to share via the sacrament in Christ's leadership over the body of the Church. Deacons and priests are ordained as cooperators with their bishop. They share in his ministry of Word, sacrament, and pastoral charity. They are not independent leaders. They are participants in the sacramental life and mission of the bishop.

The promise of obedience then expresses a commitment to a collaborative but subordinate relationship with the bishop in his threefold ministry of Word, liturgy, and pastoral charity. The ministry of preaching or celebrating sacraments is authentic to the extent that it is in communion with the bishop. The granting of faculties is not merely a juridical act. It authenticates any public proclamation of God's Word or sacramental celebration. It also means that the bishop missions the deacon or priest. It will sometimes take courage and resilience to accept these decisions, especially when a bishop does not inspire confidence by the way he fulfills his own role.

The promise of obedience goes far beyond these minimal implications. The bishop is both a father and a brother. As a father, he calls to ordination; he is the head of the ordained family; he offers pastoral care to his priests and deacons. He also lives and acts in communion with his brother bishops and in their mutual communion with the Bishop of Rome. He is called to be particularly concerned about the personal life and welfare of each priest and deacon. The priest and deacon are not to be passive in this relationship. They are expected to bring to their bishop suggestions, observations, and assistance, cooperate with him generously, correct him with charity when necessary, and truly maintain the bonds of reverence and communion.

Finally, obedience is also expressed in the way the ordained exercise authority. Those ordained are called to seek God's will before making decisions. This involves the appropriate gathering of the facts from revelation and the human situation and a genuine consultation of those to be affected by the decisions. The exercise of authority is to be a service to people, not a dominion over them.

Conclusion

The evangelical virtues of simplicity of life, celibate love, and filial obedience offer the most reliable signs that God is central in life. They also provide the most reliable route to Gospel living. They are to be lived interiorly if they are truly to shape the life of the ordained. External compliance offers just the bare minimum. Interior engagement opens up the whole Gospel way of life in relation to God, others, material possessions, and self. Bishops and priests who live these virtues from within evidence a

Gospel peace and joy that then will attract others to the message of the Gospel.

Lord God, who calls me as a disciple to live a Gospel way of life, grant that I may truly embrace simplicity of life, celibate love, and holy obedience with a generous and faithful heart. Grant this in your own name. Amen.

Chapter 16

Priests Called to Serve
in a Time of Crisis

The year 2020 was a unique year. A steady stream of new revelations about old cases of clergy sex abuse gave the impression that the Church had not really been addressing this immoral and criminal behavior effectively. COVID-19 dramatically upended everyone's life. The fiscal fallout further impoverished the poor and destabilized the lives of many who thought they were financially stable. George Floyd's horrible death in Minneapolis stirred up racial turmoil in major cities. These developments introduced significant challenges to the life and ministry of priests. Priests truly committed to the New Evangelization have had to explore innovative ways to transform these challenges into new opportunities.

The Moral Crisis of the Clergy Sex Abuse Scandal

The year 2002 had been a watershed year as the scourge of clergy sex abuse began to become public, first in Boston, then in the rest of the country. Bishops, who had been handling such cases privately, came to recognize the need to move beyond any tendency to deny or conceal the problem and to put public accountability in place. The Dallas Charter established a blueprint for each diocesan bishop to embrace: careful discernment and formation of all candidates; safe-environment training for church personnel; independent review boards to assess allegations; reports to law enforcement of all credible allegations; public disclosure to parishioners about such actions; zero tolerance of confirmed criminal behavior. In 2019 the bishops of the United States, implementing Pope Francis' motu proprio *Vos Estis Lux Mundi*, extended these policies to bishops themselves and established a national confidential vehicle for reporting suspected behavior on the part of bishops.

The most important response to this crisis, however, is not structural but spiritual. As outlined in the last two chapters, the most fruitful antidote to scandal is holiness of life and Gospel living. Priests and bishops have suffered greatly because of the sins of a few. The continuing revelations of old cases or new allegations of decades-old behavior trigger publicity that paints the Church, bishops, and priests in a painful light. This provides ample fodder for those who want to attack the Church or undermine respect for the clergy. Few people know that an annual independent audit of the Church's implementation of the 2002 initiatives and policies reports fewer than ten confirmed allegations throughout the United States every year since 2002. The latest audit available (2019) reveals that 99.98 percent of Catholic priests in America had no substantiated allegation.[1] While even one incident is always a tragedy, no institution in the world can come close to such a record.

But the greatest need, as indicated in the last chapter, is for the spiritual renewal of priests. Bishops and priests,

---

[1] *June 2020 Report on the Implementation of the Charter for the Protection of Children and Young People* (Washington, DC: USCCB Publications, 2020). (This statistic is derived from the independent StoneBridge Audit Report for 2019.)

fully embracing Gospel life, will provide the only credible witness that ordained leadership in the Church has turned a corner. It will take a radical embrace of Gospel simplicity of life, chaste celibate life and love, and joyful obedience to counteract the public image of sinfully compromised clergy. The Church needs holy priests to witness and to lead in a time of moral crisis.

The Health Crisis of COVID-19

COVID-19 and its variants have upended the lives of so many in today's world. Sickness and death as well as shut-downs and quarantines have impacted everyone in some way. The virulence and contagiousness of the virus has stirred a destabilizing fear. So many in the first world thought they were in charge of their lives. But the pandemic has brought home the truth that no one truly experiences autonomy. Life is finite and the world is sinful. However much people want to consider themselves self-sufficient in a secular world, that self-sufficiency is a sham. The world cannot save itself.

First responders became the heroes during the first months of the pandemic. Doctors, nurses, EMT person-nel, police, and firefighters moved to the front lines in the fight to serve the victimized. They worked long hours in exhausting conditions to offer emergency care to those most seriously ill or dying.

A serious question needs to be raised about the restric-tion of clergy from this front line of care. A purely secu-lar understanding of health care assumes that physical care is so important that spiritual and pastoral care are to be excluded in a time of critical needs. The scarcity of pro-tective equipment in the early days became the initial jus-tification for such exclusion. Even when dying patients or their families explicitly requested pastoral or sacramental ministry, too often this was denied them. The Church now needs to reassert in a public and persuasive way the integral nature of true health care and the critical place of the spiritual for both fostering healing and accompanying the dying.

Some dioceses formed a team of priests, who were less vulnerable to contagion and fully equipped with appropriate garb and procedures, to offer pastoral care. Authorization for such ministry was unevenly granted. Other chaplains, acting on the pastoral initiatives of Pope Francis, explored ways of reaching sickened victims through prayer cards to assist them in fostering the inner dispositions to receive God's merciful love or by using cell phones and digital devices to assist them from a distance. But much more needs to be addressed to ensure that the Church's teaching on holistic health care can guide pastoral response going forward.

Physical confinement became a significant challenge for vulnerable people seeking to protect themselves from the virus; many others faced physical confinement when shutdowns and quarantines were imposed. Most of those so confined had never experienced such extended isolation in their homes. Those addicted to feverish activity soon became stir crazy. In this imposed confinement, some parishes did become quite creative in offering opportunities for participation in live-streamed religious services and webinars or digital gatherings for inspirational instruction in the faith. In the past, busy lives seemed to keep many on the surface of life and the more tangible responsibilities in daily living. Those furloughed or restricted to on-line work at home found themselves with some time to explore the life of the spirit. This opened up for some more quiet time, more opportunities to delve into a holy reading of Sacred Scripture, and more possibilities for family prayer.

Public efforts to urge people to observe protective distancing from one another in order to reduce the transmission of the virus became framed as "social distancing". Perhaps unwittingly, this phrase fed a false impression. Yes, there was great need for "physical distancing", but this needed to be embraced together with "social solidarity". Increased time at home actually opened up rich opportunities for spending quality time together as a family. Some families rediscovered the value of the family meal, in which the activities of the day could be shared and basic virtues in human living fostered, and the importance of family prayer.

Moreover, the required distancing did not exclude creative approaches to people who were more isolated via cell phone, social media, and digital video visits. Again, more time at home did not have to lead to social isolation. There was a rich opportunity for personal care for others, utilizing the new means available today or running errands for those unable to exit their homes because of the risks to their health.

Few American Catholics ever expected to go through extended periods of time without being able to participate in Mass or receive absolution in the Sacrament of Penance and Reconciliation. This sacramental deprivation challenged both priests and people to move to a deeper spiritual engagement. In many dioceses, churches remained open for personal visits to the Blessed Sacrament. Some pastors, while closing adoration chapels, provided hours of Eucharistic adoration in the main church where participants could observe appropriate physical distancing. Most pastors live-streamed a daily Mass that remarkably often reached more people than the parishioners who usually participated in the church.

This virtual participation in Mass and the experience of spiritual communion have invited people into greater interior engagement, but they also have opened the possibility of continuing virtual participation rather than actual presence once the threats of the pandemic recede. This will require sensitive and clear instruction in the difference so that those who are able to will recognize the importance of a sacramental encounter with the Lord.

The Fiscal Crisis Caused by the Pandemic

One of the significant consequences of COVID-19 has been the economic shock it has brought to millions of people. With the shutdown of businesses, countless people have lost their jobs, others have been furloughed, and many entities forced into bankruptcy. This country has not seen such levels of unemployment since the years of the Great Depression. The poor have been hit the hardest. They have little or no resources to lean on. Those who thought their job and finances to be reasonably secure are also finding themselves drawing on savings or retirement plans to survive.

Government has an important role in trying to foster the conditions that most support the return of stable employment. Government also needs to ensure a safety net for those who are without resources through no fault of their own.

But the Church, too, has a graced opportunity to facilitate the works of mercy in service to those most in need. Catholic education, health care, and social services are even more crucial than before. In many cases it will take innovative efforts to find ways with more limited resources to continue existing service and develop new temporary initiatives. After Hurricane Katrina the Catholic schools

in New Orleans accepted public school children free of
charge when the public schools were unable to reopen
during the first year of recovery; the Daughters of Charity
created multiple health clinics when the hospitals could
not resume activities; Catholic Charities moved into mas-
sive feeding of the hungry as well as cleaning and rebuild-
ing of homes and counseling of those traumatized by the
tragedy. A human crisis invites innovative approaches to
the work of mercy.

The Church has a challenging Gospel message to break
open in a time of fiscal woe. A secular world values wealth
highly. The Gospel calls the love of it "the root of all evils"
(1 Tim 6:10). Wealth in itself is neutral. Knowing how to
use it as good stewards is crucial. Love of it as an end in itself
is lethal. The accumulation of wealth is often connected
with the pursuit of self-sufficiency. So preoccupation with
the accumulation of wealth tends to undermine faith and
trust in God's providential care for his people. Moreover,
it can close the heart to the less gifted or less fortunate. It is
a sad commentary on the behavior of wealthier people to
read the statistics that testify on an annual basis that poorer
people, percentage-wise, are far more generous with their
limited possessions than wealthy people!

The Church, too, has faced diminished financial support
in this time of economic retrenchment. It is important that
the Church be a good model for the wider society in her
care for people as she adjusts to more limited resources.

The Gospel calls disciples to trust in God, not in "horses",
the sign of greater wealth and power. The Gospel also calls
disciples to pursue the works of mercy rather than the accumulation of wealth. The Gospel calls Christians to simplicity of life rather than yielding to a consumer mentality.

In this connection, how important it is to remember that God calls his people to be good stewards of the

environment he has provided. In the Book of Genesis, it is clear that God gave human beings dominion over creation (1:28). But he also clarified that the dominion should be exercised, not by careless destruction or undisciplined consumption of the world's goods, but by cultivating and caring for them (2:15). Once again the poor often bear the brunt of the misuse of the goods of the earth.

So, Scripture offers important teaching about the role of the economy in life. The economy is to serve the human person, not the reverse. All are to be given the opportunity to participate in it. The goods of the earth are to be nurtured, not plundered. The financial system should be predicated not on getting people to buy more, but on finding better ways to provide access to the world's goods for everyone. Can this serious economic downturn lead to a fundamental reorientation of thinking, planning, and acting in the fiscal sphere?

The Social Crisis of Racial Unrest

The horrifying photos of the George Floyd death at the hands (or knee) of a uniformed Minneapolis law enforcement officer have stirred righteous indignation in the minds and hearts of most Americans. Citizens, both white and black, have marched in protest in most large cities. Some of them have become violent with rampant vandalism, arson, and direct attacks against law enforcement personnel. Peaceful protest can express righteous anger and is protected by the Constitution. Criminal conduct is not.

In this atmosphere, heated emotion needs to yield to calm reflection and responsible action. Simplistic slogans, superficial actions, or symbolic gestures can actually get in the way of the path to an effective addressing of the long-standing underlying issues. Politicizing this struggle can increase rather than decrease racist behavior in the country. The Church has a potentially significant contribution to make at this time through her teaching and through initiatives that provide conversation, friendship, and action steps toward racial harmony.

Baptism initiates all participants in a new life as sons and daughters of God the Father, brothers and sisters to one another in Christ Jesus, and temples of God's Holy Spirit. There is no more effective foundation on which to bring people together, not only in a common humanity, but in a common new life that transcends all differences. Dioceses and parishes can provide the forum where people can gather in necessary conversation and constructive initiatives that promote racial understanding, justice, and harmony. The 2018 pastoral letter of the bishops in the United States, *Open Wide Our Hearts: The Enduring Call to Love*, offers a number of concrete suggestions for accomplishing this goal.

Perhaps the most difficult and elusive challenge is to realize the conversion that all people need to undergo to make racial reconciliation and harmony possible. For whites, this conversion requires a movement from an unconscious acceptance of white privilege to Christian solidarity. For blacks, this conversion often requires a movement from an accumulated resentment to Christian charity. Neither journey is easy.

Whites do not need to be apologetic that they are white, but rather need to recognize what it means to walk in the shoes of black people. There are presumptions, courtesies, and advantages granted to whites that often are not given to blacks. Some whites may be guilty of malicious racism. But most are blind to the privileges taken for granted in daily living. Blindness is not the same as malice. But recognition of this blindness opens up the possibility of identifying small ways in which whites can unconsciously feed an experience of second-class citizenship on the part of blacks. Sins of blindness or of omission are often much more difficult to recognize and own. But this recognition can help lead to the conversion of mind, heart, and life that will most effectively promote harmony.

Blacks who experience second-class treatment can understandably develop a subtle resentment of whites. It is difficult to undergo repeated expressions of this over a lifetime. They can feel that there is an unjust need to perform better than whites in order to earn respect and equal treatment. When a particularly egregious expression of mistreatment has taken place, they can rightfully explode in anger. Anger can move in either a constructive or destructive direction. Anger in service to strong, affirming, loving action to promote goodness and righteousness is life-giving. Anger expressed in undisciplined violence against others or oneself is destructive. Often it is only heroic expressions of loving outreach on the part of whites that makes the movement from resentment to charity possible for blacks.

Tinkering with structures is easier, but ultimately less effective. The change of hearts and minds is far more challenging, but more fruitful. This is the condition for realizing a justice that promotes true reconciliation and harmony.

Conclusion

In the face of crises, the greatest temptation is to turn inward in self-protection instead of outward in self-gift. At times like these, priests experience their own vulnerability keenly. Vulnerability is actually the true state of every human being. This is hard to accept. So the human tendency is to construct a facade of being in control of life. Priests, above all, need to resist this temptation. It is actually when people most experience their vulnerability that the Good News of the *kerygma* is most readily received.

Pope Francis demonstrated this vividly in the prayer service he offered in St. Peter's Square on March 27, 2020. As the impact of COVID-19 was convulsing the world, Pope Francis moved alone into a totally abandoned square. He walked with a slight limp, a seemingly forlorn figure, unprotected from the falling rain at nightfall. Unlike Adam and Eve, who hid from God's voice when calamity descended on them, Francis moved resolutely to an improvised platform where he listened to the Word of God. The passage (Mk 4:35–41) recounted the virulent storm on the Sea of Galilee. Jesus, awakened from sleep in the stern of the boat, calmed the wind and the water and then addressed the terrified disciples: "Why are you afraid? Have you no faith?" (v. 40). In his meditative homily, Francis let those two questions reverberate throughout the square and the world—and then sat in silent absorption of those words himself. He then moved slowly to the icon *Salus Populi Romani*, as if to ask Mary for the grace to hear and respond to God's Word as she did. After veneration in silence, he moved (at Mary's bidding?) to the crucifix of the Church of San Marcello al Corso. There he paused in extended silent pondering of the mystery of Calvary and then kissed the blood-stained feet of the image of the crucified Lord. Finally, he moved to a temporary altar at the door to St. Peter's. There the Risen Lord was present in the monstrance to worship in further silence. Finally, Pope Francis wrapped his arms around the sacramental Risen Lord and raised him to the world in invitation and blessing.

Thus, in somber beauty, Pope Francis captured the vulnerability of all mankind and proclaimed the way, more in symbol than in word: come to the Lord with all that burdens; listen to his Word; hear and heed as did Mary; embrace Calvary on the way to encountering and being transformed by the Risen Lord. This moving parable in action reveals the path for priests to follow when serving the people in a time of crisis.

Lord God, I come before you with the heavy burdens that human crises always bring. Help me to listen to your Word and heed your Word; through the intercession of Mary, help me to plunge more deeply into the mystery of Calvary so as to help your people encounter more fully your life as the Risen Lord. Grant this in your own name. Amen.

Chapter 17

Renewed Priests on Fire
with the Gospel

Those who live the Gospel message then become credible witnesses to the saving and sanctifying mission of the Lord. If the Church seeks God above all, kneels in adoration before the God who saves, and evidences by a way of life that God is the route to happiness, then the Church will attract men and women, disillusioned with the false promises of a world turned in on itself.

Pope Francis, from the beginning of his pontificate, has been calling for a joyful witness to the Gospel, even to the peripheries of life.[1] While he makes this urgent call to the whole Church, he especially highlights the need for bishops and priests to point the way.[2] In a wounded Church and a broken world, the great need is for truly evangelizing bishops and priests, on fire with zeal because they have met the Lord in a transforming way and are eager to help others to meet him as well.

Encountering the Lord

How do bishops, priests, and seminary candidates meet the Lord in such a way and then continue to live in communion

---

[1] See Francis, *Evangelii Gaudium* (November 24, 2013), nos. 135–44.
[2] Ibid., no. 14.

with him? The starting point is unique for each. It may be a faith-filled home, formative experiences at school, a special moment of grace at Mass or in an adoration chapel, a moving conversion experience, a powerful retreat, a large gathering of young people engaged in prayer, song, uplifting preaching, or a transcendent moment during a tragedy. The possibilities are endless because God can use any event to break through and touch the human heart.

Holy Hour

The follow-up is what is critically important. No single encounter is going to be sufficient for a lifetime. There is no substitute for sustained quiet immersion in that experience, nurtured in regular extended prayer. Too often Christians think of prayer solely in terms of talking to God or reciting formal prayer. But God has initiated the overture of prayer. He has spoken and continues to speak. The Christian needs to grow in a capacity to listen in quiet attentiveness and receptivity. It is true that God wants his people to approach him with their needs. This expresses their rightful dependence on him. Placing their concerns in his hands, they become more open to receiving what God wants to give. An important goal of prayer is to move beyond the limitations of self-will toward acceptance of God's will, "not what I will, but what you will" (Mk 14:36).

The Second Vatican Council urges those called to Holy Orders to recognize that the very ministry in which they are engaged challenges them to an ever deeper interior life. Thus, the ministry of the Word calls for thoughtful and prayerful preaching. The ordained cannot preach or teach the Word of God with fidelity, insight, and depth without listening to that Word and pondering that Word regularly in prayer. That is why they pledge to pray the Liturgy of Hours each day. They are to become men of prayer, nourished by Sacred Scripture and Holy Tradition, for the sake of the people. *Lectio divina*, then, is not an option. It is the ordinary way for priests to meet the Lord daily, open themselves to him, and be formed by him. This takes regular quiet time, because praying the Hours quickly, routinely, or superficially will not make that possible. If those committed to the Liturgy of Hours commit themselves to quiet prayer for an hour each day and incorporate some portion of the Office in that prayer, they are more likely to become true men of prayer. This interior engagement with the Word of God will gradually impact the public proclamation of God's Word and help the preacher discover blessed ways of helping listeners to become more attentive to God's Word as well. And, in a particular way, the Psalms will come alive as graced vehicles for lifting up the sufferings, anxieties, fears, and joy of the people.

The Mysteries of Faith

The Second Vatican Council declares the Sacred Liturgy to be "the source and summit of the Christian life".[3] Once again for this objective truth to become subjectively true for the people, those celebrating the Liturgy must become interiorly engaged in this ministry. The Mass is not just a ceremony or a worship service. It is the representation in sacrament of the redemptive Mystery of Faith. What happened on Calvary was an historical expression of the Son's loving, sacrificial response to his Father in the Holy Spirit

[3] *Lumen Gentium*, no. 11, in *The Documents of Vatican II*, ed. Walter M. Abbot, trans. Joseph Gallagher (St. Louis, MO: Herder and Herder, 1966).

for our salvation. This pivotal event in all human history becomes present and accessible to everyone in this great sacrament. What a privilege to be invited! What an awesome role to enact it in Christ's name! In the ordination ceremony, the bishop admonishes the priest, just ordained with the laying on of hands and consecratory prayer, to accept the paten and chalice with the gifts of bread and wine, in these words: "Understand what you do, imitate what you celebrate and conform your life to the mystery of the Lord's cross."[4]

How does the priest nourish the appropriate awe to celebrate the Sacred Mysteries well? The Liturgical Instruction for the Roman Missal urges the priest to prepare with recollection, to celebrate prayerfully by observing the moments of silence that the liturgical directives prescribe, and to preserve time afterward to commune with the sacramental Lord humbly and gratefully. If a priest can engage in his hour of personal prayer in the presence of the Blessed Sacrament, this will foster not only communion with God but also an ever deeper awe and reverence in the presence of the sacrament of the altar.

This same interior engagement in the celebration of each of the other sacraments helps to foster the sanctification of both the celebrant and those who receive them. For instance, the celebration of the Sacrament of Penance and Reconciliation offers a unique way to foster continuing conversion of life and help those in need of a more radical conversion in their lives. Some people need to grow in conversion; some people need fundamental reconciliation as well. Both Pope St. John Paul II and Pope Francis have proclaimed that the greatest need in the world today

---

[4] *The Roman Pontifical*, "Ordination of Priests", second typical edition (Washington, DC: USCCB Publications, 2003), n. 135.

is for mercy. God reveals himself in the Scriptures as the God of mercy. Salvation history is an account of God's repeated offers of Divine Mercy. In the hour of his most intense suffering on the Cross, Jesus prayed to his Father for the forgiveness of all who inflicted that excruciating death upon him. He even offered it personally to a rebel thief dying with him on a cross. Mercy was and is the Lord's mission!

The priest is ordained to be a minister of that mercy in the name of Christ. If he is to be a good confessor, he needs to be a good penitent first. As St. John Chrysostom taught, only those who engage in the spiritual struggle for virtue and against vice are going to be able to help penitents to do the same. How important it is for the priest to signal by his preaching, availability, and his own example that this ministry holds a high priority in his life. Conversion is a lifelong journey. Progress is usually quite gradual. But fidelity to it leads to humility before God, patience with self, and compassion for others.

Pastoral Agape

The Second Vatican Council also taught that pastoral care is a source of spirituality. This, too, depends on interior engagement. St. Gregory the Great admonished the priest always to be faithful to the Gospel teaching, but to recognize that people need to hear that teaching adapted to the temperament, vices, virtues, opportunities, and circumstances of their lives. It is easy just to quote the teaching on the one hand or to accommodate the teaching on the other. It takes prayerful discernment to identify which facets of the teaching need to be accentuated in order for the person to mature in Christian response to the Gospel.

How does the priest see Christ in those whom he is offering the spiritual or corporal works of mercy? It takes prayerful meditation or consideration as St. Bernard counseled Pope Eugene III. Christ reveals his face in every person in need of pastoral care. But that face is recognized only if the priest is daily seeking the face of the Lord. The test is greatest when the need for pastoral care is most unexpected or inconvenient. Virtue grows most when tested.

Developments in the Formation of Priests

There are some helpful developments in the norms that the Church has recently promulgated for the formation of priests. The *Ratio Fundamentalis*[5] to guide seminary formation no longer treats progress toward ordination with a primary focus on the fulfillment of academic requirements, but rather on a more holistic consideration of the gradual maturation of candidates. It first identifies a Propaedeutic Stage in which there is careful discernment of the qualifications that make acceptance into seminary advisable. This discernment includes attention to human and faith growth and proper motivation, both of which are foundational for serious considerations of candidates for the priesthood.

Then a second step, called the Discipleship Stage, begins with acceptance into either a college seminary or a pre-theology program. In this stage, the candidate pursues not only liberal arts with a major focus on philosophy but also a basic exposure to the teaching of the Church, rooted in but not confined to the *Catechism of the Catholic Church*. But the overriding purpose of this stage is to assist

[5] Congregation for the Clergy, *The Gift of the Priestly Vocation: Ratio Fundamentalis Institutionis Sacerdotalis*, in *L'Osservatore Romano*, December 8, 2016.

the candidate to become a true disciple of the Lord. He is to enter into an ever deeper encounter with the Lord that not only begins to transform him but also leads him to want to hand his life over to the Lord. For this to happen, the candidate needs to experience a conversion from a self-centered approach to life toward a greater capacity for self-gift. He needs to grow in a capacity for sustained personal prayer, deeper engagement in the sacramental life of the Church, and growth in virtue. This step should ultimately culminate in a fundamental vocational decision, both personal and ecclesial, which recommends admission to candidacy.

The next step, the Configuration Stage, plunges the student into all the theological studies he needs to become an informed and responsible pastoral minister; the principal purpose of this stage is to ensure that the candidate is growing in his embrace of the significant virtues that marked the Lord's public ministry. Growing knowledge of the content of faith needs to be integrated into the life of prayer and initial experience in pastoral ministry. The goal is to grow in uniting himself with the mind and heart of Christ—Head, Shepherd, and Bridegroom of his Church. This stage culminates in ordination to the diaconate.

The next step, called the Stage of Pastoral Integration, begins in the diaconal internship and continues into priestly life and ministry after ordination to the priesthood. The challenge at this step revolves around ensuring that human maturity, academic learning, and progress in the spiritual journey coalesce in shaping good pastoral ministry. Although there is special focus on this during the diaconal internship, this ongoing challenge continues into and throughout priestly life and ministry.

This focus both on reaching appropriate benchmarks during each stage and on ensuring that maturation is occurring concomitantly on the human, intellectual, spiritual, and pastoral levels means that the focus is to be no longer primarily on academic performance, but on the integrated maturation of the seminarian. This means that all engaged in the work of formation—bishop, vocation director, seminary rector, formation advisors, professors, spiritual directors, and parish supervisors—are to collaborate in fostering a united effort in priestly formation. In this way, even though each has unique gifts and responsibilities to bring to this collaborative venture, all share a common commitment to ensure that the human, intellectual, faith, and moral virtues needed for good pastoral ministry are being fostered.

Zeal for Evangelization

Since the ministerial priesthood is in service to the baptismal priesthood, the ordained priest needs to embrace the most pressing challenge in the Church today: helping people to encounter the Lord themselves. So many hunger for God but do not know for whom they are hankering or how to meet him.

So, they need to meet witnesses who are obviously in love with the Lord, and who also want to help them meet the Lord. Joyful, loving priests attract those who are seeking or those who are discouraged by a chaotic world. When people meet priests who are able to preach the Gospel message with credibility because of the way they live, they will often find themselves experiencing what Augustine found in Ambrose in Milan. When people meet priests who celebrate the Sacred Mysteries with interior awe and reverence, they will be drawn to the kind of spiritual experience that led Thomas Aquinas to consider all else that he had written as straw in comparison. When people

meet priests who love them with a saving and sanctifying
love, they will experience a contemporary Gregory who
invites them to seek not what pleases their fallen human
inclinations but what appeals to their deeper aspirations.

Priests who are humanly mature, intellectually alert,
inquisitive, and spiritually alive will explore every avenue to help people meet the Lord in a meaningful and
life-changing way. For some, it will be helping them to
encounter the Lord in personal prayer; for others it will
be in participation in the Eucharist or in the quiet of
Eucharistic adoration; for still others it may be in a retreat.
Many are helped by a group experience wherein they are
joined with peers in listening to a convinced and con-
vincing proclamation of the Word and in experiencing
others committed to the Lord. Some are helped through
the service of those in need, shaped by Gospel formation.
Many young people live their lives on social media and
sometimes can manifest a remarkable openness to engagement in the search for God on that media. Moreover, it
is imperative that all religious education be in the form of
an evangelizing catechesis. Unless young people meet the
Lord, they will not desire to learn his message.

Evangelizing the Culture

The evangelization needed today includes realism about
the culture. As Francis Cardinal George perceptively commented, missionaries cannot evangelize either a people or a
culture they do not love.[6] "For God," as St. John testified,

---

[6] See Francis Cardinal George, O.M.I., *The Difference God Makes: A Catholic Vision of Faith, Communion, and Culture* (New York: Crossroad Publishing,
2009), Chap. 2.

"sent the Son into the world, not to condemn the world, but that the world might be saved through him" (3:17).

The mature, loving evangelizer needs to remember St. Gregory the Great's focus on good discernment in responsible pastoral outreach. In our culture and in the people who live in our culture are both the seeds of the Word of God and the seeds of the Enemy. In his parable of the wheat and the weeds (Mt 13:24–30), the Lord Jesus urged caution. If those witnessing to the Gospel become overly focused on uprooting the weeds, they can unwittingly uproot the wheat.

So, it is important first to identify some of the seeds of the Word of God that people in the United States tend to absorb from the culture. Americans tend to value equality, freedom, openness, participation in decision-making, an entrepreneurial spirit, freedom of speech, tolerance, openness to the future, and human rights. There is no question that there are seeds of the Gospel in each of these.

Each of these values, however, can be distorted. Equality, which rightly acknowledges a shared and common human dignity, can be interpreted as meaning a false egalitarianism that dismisses legitimate human difference, even those as fundamental as the ones that differentiate male and female. Freedom, which truly increases with choices for the good and the true, can too easily be invoked in support of moral license or blatant falsehoods. Are people more free if they choose a lie over truth? The rightful desire for appropriate openness can unveil hidden corruption. But when the demand for openness undermines professional confidentiality, or even the seal of confession, the basic trust needed in human relationships and religious freedom can be undermined. A respect for rightful participation in decision-making can also be subverted by a demand that what is right or wrong be determined by a plebiscite.

Similarly, a wholesome promotion of the entrepreneur-ial spirit can give rise to wonderful new initiatives for the common good, or it can lead people to think that every new discovery is an unmitigated good. A commitment to free speech provides the possibility for a healthy exchange of ideas. It can also provide an unregulated platform for vitriol, pornographic seduction, and the promotion of violence. When the encouragement of tolerance is rooted in our God-given responsibility to love one another, even our enemies, it is life-giving. When tolerance leads to the acceptance of horrible evil, it is misguided. Openness to the future allows for authentic growth and development; but it can also be corrupted to promote a disdain for les-sons that should be learned from the past. A respect for human rights makes possible a wholesome respect. But when people create new rights, not rooted in nature but rather in contemporary opinions, such as *political correctness*, then they confuse what human rights really are.

It is obvious, then, that good evangelizers need spiritual discernment in order to witness to the Gospel responsibly and fruitfully. St. Ignatius of Loyola has taught us that the principle and foundation for good discernment is to seek God, his truth, and his goodness above all while becom-ing detached from everything or anything that stands in the way. These twin conditions point to the deepest yearning in the human heart for God as well as the real obstacles we experience in our fallen human nature. It requires spiritual and moral maturity to embrace those conditions as operating virtues guiding our approach to the pastoral challenges. This approach helps us to avoid two extremes: one, the inclination to position ourselves as simply *countercultural*, thus becoming negative or hyper-critical; the other, the inclination simply to *accommodate* to the culture uncritically.

Moreover, it is important to remember that the culture is not just the external environment in which people live and labor, but a reality that shapes even the evangelizer as well. For instance, digital technology now permeates the culture. It offers significant opportunities to learn, to communicate, and to fulfill work responsibilities. It can also trap people into an overload of superficial information or divisive rhetoric that makes personal communion with God and one another more challenging. Moreover, indulgence in the digital world can rob people of the inner silence needed to focus on what is more lasting in life. It takes discernment to utilize social media creatively in order to reach those not actively engaged in Church life and faith, while not succumbing to the emotionally charged ideologically laced postings that undermine civil public discourse.

It is also important to recognize that the relationships that social media nurtures are virtual rather than real. People who become addicted to virtual connectivity can lose a needed facility in fostering human relationships. If preoccupation with digital communication undermines human communion, it will be necessary to adopt an appropriate self-discipline in its use.

Parresia

The core message for those who evangelize must be the basic *kerygma* of the Gospel: God has created every human being; he sustains each in existence; even after the original fall and personal sin, he offers redemption in Christ Jesus; this Lord and Savior died for our sins and rose for our justification; nothing is more important than eternal salvation and life with him forever. The kingdom of God is at hand. Repent and believe the Good News!

This is not a time for the mere maintenance of parishes. This is a time for releasing the power of the Holy Spirit. Parishes need to approach all of their ministries through the prism of evangelization. For the Church is not Church unless she is missionary in outreach and zeal.

Nor is this a time for the timid! The Holy Spirit has given the gift of *parresia* in the laying on of hands. It will require wisdom, conviction, courage, even boldness to reproclaim the Gospel in our own time.

So, who are going to be good apostles today? Is it not going to be those who have turned their lives over to the Lord, who live the Gospel way of life, who have explored the way in which God's revelation interacts with the real issues of today's society, who can relate maturely and humanly with fellow pilgrims, and who are on fire with the zeal of the Lord?

There is no substitute for daily communion with the One to whom priests have consecrated their lives and love. There is a pressing need to continue to penetrate the mysteries of faith. There has to be an eagerness to understand better the challenges people face and the issues that underlie them. As living instruments of God, priests have to be at home in their humanity, self-disciplined, and self-giving. They must also be on fire for the Lord and his saving, sanctifying mission. When these gifts flourish in her priests, the Church comes alive with an attractive joy.

Mary, Mother of Priests

If priests and bishops are being called to reveal Christ to the world, to embrace a Gospel way of life, and to proclaim the Gospel message with zeal and courage, there is no better person to whom to turn than Mary. Mary was the first to present Christ to this world. She embraced a profound simplicity of life. She consecrated herself to virginal love. She surrendered her will to God in her "let it be to me according to your word" (Lk 1:38). In her Magnificat (Lk 1:46–55), Mary uttered the most powerful proclamation of the Gospel message to the world.

It was especially at the foot of the Cross that Mary revealed her priestly heart. She united her pierced heart with that of her Son's as she offered herself in union with his self-sacrifice. Then at his bidding, she accepted every disciple as sons or daughters in her Son. So, she became both the model for and the Mother of all priests.

Mary, model and Mother of all priests, intercede with your Son, that the Church may know more and more missionary disciples, apostolic missionaries, and joyful evangelizing priests in a wounded Church and a broken world. God grant this through your Son and our Lord, Jesus Christ. Amen.

POSTSCRIPT ON CLERICALISM

The clergy abuse scandal has triggered a new focus on the issue of clericalism. It is obvious that people differ in their definition of clericalism. Fundamentally, it is a corruption of the very purpose of Holy Orders. But it is important first and foremost to recognize that the vocation to be a cleric is profoundly good! Men are ordained to the clerical state because the Church has discerned that Christ has chosen them (*kleroein*) to represent him in the Sacrament of Holy Orders. What a great grace that is! Those who succumb to clericalism use the office to serve *themselves* rather than *the Lord*. That is the issue!

In a wider context, clericalism is a form of narcissism. Narcissists are immature and tend to think that the world should serve them. It is appropriate for babies to expect that the world revolves around them, but not adults. Narcissists, then, use people and things around them to satisfy their own immature, egotistical needs.

The Lord has invited his disciples to a *much more* noble way of life. When Christ spelled out the cost of discipleship, he declared that only those who prefer *him* to people (including even family members), possessions, and their own lives in this world are worthy to be his disciple (Lk 14:26–27; cf. Mt 16:24–28; Mk 8:34–38; Lk 9:23–27). He selected his apostles from among such disciples.

Discipleship, then, frees a man to become a good cleric, whereas clericalism is directly opposed to it. Clericalism can play out in a sense of entitlement regarding material possessions, in manipulative relationships of other people, and in an immature submission to authority on the one hand and then an egotistical exercise of authority on the other hand when assuming office. It will be helpful to look at each of these.

Entitlement is rooted in a false conviction that the Church owes a cleric special treatment because of his state of life. He expects support for a comfortable life, gifts, freebies, meals, treats, and vacation opportunities usually available only to those more financially well off. He can become focused on externals in vestments, ceremonies, and the trappings of office rather than the interior life. To wear clerical garb in order to seek favored treatment or to cover for immaturity is wrong. To wear clerical garb to signal consecration to the Lord and availability for service to others, especially regarding their salvation and sanctification, is great!

Manipulation of others expresses itself in false friendships. The priest may seek worldly advantage through friendship: admission to more elite social circles, special treatment in social activities, privileges not available to most people—and often isolation from the poor and needy. It is especially troublesome when a priest seeks gratification through the manipulation of others in immoral sexual behavior. So, when the collar invites trust because one's life is primarily lived for God, wonderful. But when the collar is self-serving, it is a counter sign and a betrayal.

Egotism, although present in a priest's inappropriate pursuit of both material gratification and personal advantage, can be most evident in relation to authority. A priest can try to compensate for his own immaturity by cultivating favor with authority figures but criticizing them behind their back. Then, when exercising authority he can use his office to exercise control over others. This expresses itself in an authoritarian exercise of power over laity in general, women and subordinates in particular. It is marked by discomfort with genuine consultation and decision-making in service to one's own goals rather than the common good. Such priests can shun ambiguity and, therefore, apply rules rigidly. Yes, the cleric is entrusted with authority, but it is an authority that always points to Christ and is expressed in *service*. The ordained priesthood is in service to baptismal priesthood. He is called to proclaim the Church's faith and moral teaching with authority. He is called to witness rather than condemn, to propose rather than impose.

The Church has struggled with clericalism from the beginning. Even though Jesus had spelled out the cost of discipleship multiple times, Simon Peter one moment accepted the Lord's promise to make his faith the "rock" (Mt 16:18) on which the Church would be built—and then moments later rejected the Lord's impending suffering and Death as integral to that very faith which was to be the "rock" for the Church (vv. 21–23). He also denied even knowing the Lord to escape arrest himself after the Lord was taken into custody in Gethsemane. James and John, coached by their mother, sought the first places in the kingdom. So Jesus had to clarify that the exercise of authority in the Church was to be done as he exercised it. He came to serve, not to be served (Mt 20:20–28; Mk 10:35–45). Judas so succumbed to greed for a comfortable life at the expense of the poor that he ended up betraying the Lord (Mt 26:14–16; Mk 14:10–11; Lk 22:3–6) and then despaired of forgiveness and committed suicide (Mt 27:3–10).

As soon as the Church emerged from the catacombs after the initial centuries of persecution, St. John Chrysostom in the East (in his treatise on *The Priesthood*) and St. Augustine in the West (*Homily on Ezekiel* 34) used strong language in denouncing clericalism as a false accommodation to the world. They did not use the word "clericalism", but they denounced all forms of narcissism in the ordained and held up the evangelical virtues to counteract this kind of behavior.

In each subsequent era when the Church struggled with the need to bring renewal to the priesthood, she has turned to the evangelical virtues to point the way. Simplicity of life enables the disciple to treat material possessions as gifts to use insofar as they help him fulfill his responsibilities in his vocation and to let go of them when they get in the way. Chaste life and love (in celibacy for priests) enables the disciple to respect the dignity of others and counteracts any tendency to use others inappropriately to satisfy one's own needs. Obedience enables the disciple to submit his egotistical self-will to God through legitimate superiors and to exercise authority as a true servant.

Thus, the evangelical virtues, embraced inwardly, generously, and faithfully, are the God-given antidotes to clericalism. These three virtues counteract the threefold vices that lead to clericalism.

Could it also be true that these same evangelical virtues are the answer to at least some expressions of contemporary anti-clericalism? Anti-clericalism moves beyond rejecting clerical vices to rejecting the Sacrament of Holy Orders itself. But when people experience priests truly living a simplicity of life, chaste celibate love, and obediential service, prejudices against the role of priests tend to dissipate and the Gospel message comes alive.

This Gospel-inspired way of life leads to joyful priests, alive to evangelical living and afire with the Gospel message in the Church and for the world!

ACKNOWLEDGMENTS

No one can write a book alone. Books emerge from communities. This one is rooted in the classical spiritual communion of the Roman Catholic Church and the experience of teaching a course to seminarians at Notre Dame Seminary in New Orleans.

The special challenges of the clergy sex abuse scandal and the sometimes inept way in which some bishops have handled it provided the initial impetus for a book that would address the priestly moral and spiritual renewal so much needed in the Church today. Then the events of 2020 brought the need for renewal into even sharper focus. Efforts at priestly renewal in the past can help us appreciate the way forward now.

After preparing a draft, I tested it with some friends and collaborators who agreed to read it critically and make suggestions. I am deeply indebted to Monsignor Cornelius McRae; Sister Evelyn Ronan, S.N.D.; Very Reverend James Wehner; Reverend Joseph Krafft; Dr. Thomas Neal; and Dr. Rebecca Maloney for their thoughtful and helpful suggestions. Where I was able to incorporate their observations, they enriched the text.

I am particularly appreciative that Bishop Robert Barron was willing to provide the encouraging Foreword. I have admired his gift for evangelization for some time. In these last few years, I have come to treasure his episcopal ministry, leadership, and friendship.

Mrs. Patricia Elton Annoni has given countless hours and painstaking effort to the technical preparation of the manuscript. I stand daily in her debt for her patience, her competence, and the loving care with which she has offered this valued service.

God grant that this work may in some small way serve the renewal he calls us priests to embrace in the service to the priesthood of the faithful.

ART CREDITS

Chapter 1	Courtesy of National Gallery of Art, Washington
Chapter 2	Courtesy of Rijksmuseum, Amsterdam
Chapter 3	Courtesy of Rijksmuseum, Amsterdam
Chapter 4	Courtesy of National Gallery of Art, Washington
Chapter 5	Courtesy of Rijksmuseum, Amsterdam
Chapter 6	Courtesy of Rijksmuseum, Amsterdam
Chapter 7	Courtesy of National Gallery of Art, Washington
Chapter 8	Courtesy of National Gallery of Art, Washington
Chapter 9	Courtesy of Rijksmuseum, Amsterdam
Chapter 10	Courtesy of Rijksmuseum, Amsterdam
Chapter 11	Farabola/Bridgeman Images
Chapter 12	Everett Collection/Bridgeman Images
Chapter 13	Alessia Pierdomenico/Shutterstock.com
Chapter 14	Giulio Napolitano/Shutterstock.com
Chapter 15	AM113/Shutterstock